SO IT GOES

SO IT GOES

Travels in the Aran Isles, Xian and places in between

NICOLAS BOUVIER

Translated by
Robyn Marsack

ELAND
London

First published in French under the titles
Journal d'Aran et d'autres lieux, *Voyage dans les Lowlands*
and *Thesaurus Pauperus ou la guerre à huit ans*

First published in Great Britain by Eland Publishing Ltd
61 Exmouth Market, London EC1R 4QL in 2019
with the support of the Swiss Arts Council Pro Helvetia

Journal d'Aran et d'autres lieux © Éditions Payot, 1989
Éditions Payot & Rivages, 2015
Voyages dans les Lowlands and *Dans les brumes de l'île du whisky*
© Éliane Bouvier
Thesaurus Pauperus ou la guerre à huit ans © Éditions Zoé, 1999
Translation and introductory passages © Robyn Marsack, 2019

ISBN 978 1 78060 114 4

Text set in England by James Morris
Printed in England by Clays Ltd, Elcograf S.p.A.

Contents

Publisher's Foreword

Only twice have I read a travel book and immediately wanted to speak to the author. The first time it was Ogier de Busbecq's *Turkish Letters*, and I was well aware that I would never get through to the sixteenth-century Habsburg ambassador to the court of Suleyman the Magnificent. The second time was when I finished *The Way of the World* by Nicolas Bouvier in 2006. It didn't take long to discover that Bouvier had died in 1998, and I entered a period of mourning for this man I had never met.

Despite his brilliance, Bouvier had largely slipped back beneath the Anglophone waves. Tracking down and publishing the works which had been translated – *The Way of the World*, *The Japanese Chronicles* and *The Scorpion-Fish* – allowed me to spend time with his words if nothing else. I tried, and largely failed, to trace the field recordings he had made of music from Zagreb to Tokyo. I looked at the images he had collected from around the world, the photographs he began to take in Japan in the 1960s, the poetry he wrote. I watched, much more than once, the film made about him in 1993, *Le hibou et la baleine*, and other snippets on the internet. I still long to have met him, and feel quite envious of the translator of these stories, who did.

So It Goes is the final element of Eland's homage to this exceptional chronicler of the world – a selection of his shorter pieces of travel writing, and an essay on the childhood which catapulted him into the world equipped with such fertile curiosity. It contains all the hallmarks of his particular genius: an acute, painterly eye for the details which escape many others, an ear attuned as much to the qualities of a wind or the soft exhalation of a carthorse as to the nuances of conversation, and a willingness to open himself totally to the experience of a place, even when it threatens to unhinge him.

The title, *So It Goes*, is a phrase which crops up like a mantra throughout the book. Bouvier borrowed it from Kurt Vonnegut, whose writing he hugely admired. In *Slaughterhouse Five* (1969), the phrase implies that even faced with the horrific destruction of war, no good will come of shirking the truth. Bouvier is as good as his word.

Rose Baring
London, 2019

Acknowledgements

The publishers and translator acknowledge the following publications, from which quotations have been taken:

Kings, Lords and Commons: Irish Poems from the Seventh Century to the Nineteenth Century, translated with a preface by Frank O'Connor (Dublin: Gill and Macmillan, 1959), for 'The End of Clonmacnoise', Anon.; *Alcools* by Guillaume Apollinaire (Berkeley & LA: University of California Press, 1965) for the quotation from 'Le Larron', which is adapted from the translation by Anne Hyde Guest; *Collected Poems* Vol. 1 by Michael Hartnett (Dublin/Manchester: Raven Arts/Carcanet Press, 1984/5) for the lines from 'A Small Farm'; *Collected Poems* by John Montague (Oldcastle: The Gallery Press, 1995) for the lines from 'Patriotic Suite': 'The gloomy images of a provincial Catholicism'.

The translator gratefully acknowledges support from the Royal Literary Fund while working on this translation; Rose Baring's enthusiasm and editorial skills; the help of Anna Crowe, whose eagle eye and poet's sensibility were invaluable; the encouragement of Diana Hendry; and suggestions from Andrew Rubens on the last lap.

If you don't find the ordinary supernatural,
what's the good of carrying on?

Charles-Albert Cingria, *La Fourmi Rouge*

Aran Journal

Everything red is beautiful
everything new is fair
everything high is lovely
everything common is bitter
everything we lack is prized [...]

The Sickbed of Cuchulain
or *The Wasting Sickness of Cuchulain*
Trinity College MS

Nicolas Bouvier conceded that the price you pay for leading a nomadic life in the open air is the sacrifice of the things that go with a civil servant's career, such as paid holidays, a pension, retirement. 'All the same,' he said to his interviewer Irene Lichtenstein-Fall, 'it is an incredible freedom to live as I've been able to live.' The days that he spent on Aran were governed by the winter weather and the illness he had contracted on the mainland. Back in Geneva, Bouvier took to his bed for three weeks, but on the island he kept walking – 'I had to get material for my article' – and lived on 'sea-air and wind'. Indeed, he declared that the wind was the main character in the Aran Journal. *In their discussion of belief in the supernatural, his elderly host also emerged as an important element of the stay. As Bouvier said, 'Obviously in that extreme weather and with a fever, when someone is constantly telling you stories about fairies, you are more likely to believe in them than if you are in good health, with a pastis in front of you in Aix-les-Bains.'*

Clonmacnoise
February 1985

The river coils and winds just below fields white with ice. It is bordered by willows and recumbent sheep, which allow you to guess its path, unpredictable as rivers are: one more meander is what a river does best; indeed, that's just what we expect.

The narrow, blue road, shining with ice, also winds without rhyme or reason where it could run straight, and takes the hillocks it should avoid at as steep an angle as possible. It goes its own way. The sky, powered by a fresh westerly, is a hard blue. The cold – minus fifteen degrees – grips the whole countryside in its clenched fist. Driving is very slow; I have all the time in the world.

'What news from Clonmacnoise?' the poet asks a student:

'How are things keeping there?'
'Oh, things are shaping fair –
Foxes round churchyards bare
Gnawing the guts of men.'

(Anon., eleventh century)

The road abuts a wall as it climbs: behind it are an infinite number of grey stone crosses, mossy, lying down, standing up, planted all askew in mown grass of an indescribable green. To the west, the grave-strewn field descends towards a tower shaped like a pencil and served by one opening, four metres off the ground. When the Norsemen or Vikings were scouring the countryside, the monks took refuge there, hauled up the ladder and lost themselves in useless prayer. The pagans surrounded the refuge, which hummed with anxious voices; they lit bundles of well-dried brambles and smoked out the besieged like so many badgers, while getting hopelessly drunk. What gales of laughter there must have been below. Lower down, the River Shannon carries chunks of ice around a bend. The frozen rose gardens whistle in a squall. The wind tears from the river scarves of water that sting my face. Between this tower, these

13

graves, and the stumps of several destroyed Romanesque churches, you can see sheep grazing – or rather, woolly zeppelins, with their silly narrow heads above such spindly legs that anywhere else they would have been carried away like snowflakes. Not here. This is no ordinary place: like Delphi, like holy Isé, it is a charged, serious site, with its special guardians, its own history.

Everything begins in the fifth century on the isle of Inishmore off the west of Ireland, where St Enda cemented his Christian faith by fasting and mortification. He would lie face down in prayer for hours on end, in a dry-stone hermitage which you would not use as a pigsty, exposed to the bitter winter weather. In 545 his disciple St Ciaran, who had been raised in this hard school, returned to the mainland and founded the Abbey of Clonmacnoise beside a creek, on the river which at that time was the only communication route in the country. He was under the protection of a clan chief, to whom he promised the crown of Ireland – he made good his promise – and who helped him put the first beam in place. There is a great stone cross here, eroded by the wind, on which you can still make out the king and the saint staggering under the weight of an oak joist. The same year St Ciaran took to his bed, confided to the monks around it, 'Awful is the way to the world beyond,' and passed away. I believe him and his frankness pleases me: it takes character not to lie at that moment. A century and a half later Clonmacnoise, with its two thousand monks and monklings, was the largest abbey in Europe, one of the hubs of Christianity, the source of preaching that would spread everywhere. The monastic rule left by St Ciaran is the severest of all: meditation, silence, vast amounts of reading, eye-popping transcription duties, back-breaking woodcutting duties, a little bad beer when the bells rang on the great feast days. When they were actually permitted, celebrations were shattering. The abbey was hugely wealthy: the skeletons of a hundred and thirteen sheep were buried under one yew tree struck by lightning in 1149. At that period there were three churches, windmills, sheepfolds, wine cellars, laundries, refectories, stables, a scriptorium for illuminating manuscripts, a port and fishponds on the Shannon. This excited the envy of Norsemen, Vikings and rival Irish tribes, the 'foxes' of the poet's words. Between the seventh and the fifteenth centuries the abbey was pillaged, burnt and razed twenty times, and rebuilt twenty times. Then this tremendous energy withered away and became feeble: for eight hundred years the Irish had given their all, had undertaken too much; they are still recovering even as I write.

In the seventeenth century, when Cromwell passed through in search of bits of wall to knock down – as was his hobby – there wasn't much left to destroy. What remains is this mysterious forest of toppling Celtic crosses, where the plots have always been coveted – St Ciaran declared that hell would never know the dead of Clonmacnoise – and obtained through a system of familial and territorial privilege so complicated that even the most accomplished procedural lawyers in the country lost their learned way among the thorns. In any case, the few epitaphs in the old cemetery that can still be deciphered do not cause any concern as to the salvation of those who rest here. In the winter of 1985, only one person enjoyed the privilege: a lady of ninety-nine, because she was born in the county of Offaly. For thirty years, the 'new dead' have been buried in a cemetery adjoining the abbey grounds, without any celestial guarantee, and in graves in the style of the day, which is to say hideous.

When, from the seventh century, this ardent, demanding, stubborn Christianity, enhanced by wonders which remind us of those of Tibetan lamas or Mongolian shamans, returned to the Continent like a boomerang borne on the evangelical zeal of these athletes of God – these champions of fasting – it did not appeal to everyone. This brave cutting taken from a distant miracle, this Christ fresh as a hawthorn whom the Irish monks addressed familiarly and called 'the Great Abbot', this asceticism with a touch of wizardry, was received with the greatest reservations by the cardinals in their scarlet and the Roman prelates fed on Judaeo-Latin legalism, pork pâté and Frascati. The strident green of the shamrock or the darker Celtic mistletoe clashed somewhat with the background of faded episcopal or Pompeian red. Irish monasticism was very egalitarian – St Ciaran was the son of a cartwright – and unconcerned with pontifical hierarchy. Besides, these druid-saints have the devil's own cheek, and 'powers' which perhaps they owe to the Spartan rigour of their apprenticeship to God. It's impossible to see the anchorites' cells on the Skellig or Aran islands – sties open to the winds off the Atlantic, so low that you have to crawl to enter them – without being reminded of the testing years of the Tibetan magician Milarepa, who could turn rain into hail if he pleased, and decapitate all the wedding guests at a feast two hours away – as the crow flies – to show his displeasure. One of these Irishmen – I can't remember now which one – is said to have crossed the sea in a stone trough paddling with his hands, sign of a sturdy faith. In short, these men mad for God are frightening.

Undoubtedly St Gall and St Columbanus would have passed through Clonmacnoise, if only for a hurried meal, in their haste to reach the French coast and throw their punches. Hardly did they disembark before things began to go sour. In Burgundy, where they reprimanded the barons over their concubines, their bastards and above all – and this was too much – their gluttony, they were asked to clear off. They went north as far as Lake Constance, and threw the most sacred idols of the Suevi tribe into the lake. That, also, was too much. They fled, and separated. St Columbanus nipped over the Alpine passes to Italy, where he founded the Abbey at Bobbio. St Gall took refuge in a wild little valley west of the lake, the domain of bears. He got rid of them by wielding his sprinkler of holy water, but it was a sprinkler conditioned by a Celtic sensibility, always ready to negotiate with nature, its vagaries and its spokesmen. Where there is power, even a bear – we might say especially a bear – will bend. This is how the chronicler Walafrid, two centuries later, tells the story of the eviction:

> But a bear came down from the mountains, approached their campfire and carefully collected the scraps they had let fall. Seeing this, the man of God said to the beast: 'I command you in the name of the Lord to get a branch and lay it on the fire.' Lo and behold, the bear obeyed, searching out a fallen branch and putting it on the fire. Then the saint rummaged in his bag and brought out a loaf of bread, gave it to the bear and said, 'In the name of the Lord, leave this valley and return to the mountains...'

Appreciating what he was dealing with better than the Pope of Rome, the bear did as he was told, not out of fear but because he had a proper understanding of such powers, of their presence and their weight. Having also chased away from the river bank two she-devils who had provoked him with their nudity, St Gall went on to found an abbey which would become as powerful as Clonmacnoise and above all, the centre of the revival of plainsong in Christendom, thanks to a new system of musical notation – neumes. This revival was essential because the Christianised barbarians had completely distorted the music of the liturgy 'with their Alpine roughness… their raucous voices growling like thunder… their throats hot with drink', as a Roman precentor wrote, having a good laugh over the chanting of these loudmouths…

Day begins to wane, the shadows of the crosses lengthen. The light has plummeted; it is so cold that I have to warm my camera between my shirt and my thighs so that the shutter consents to work.

At the entrance to the cemetery, in a log cabin still oozing resin, I find a young man who is both guardian and historian of the dead. He offers me tea and a brochure he has written on the history of the abbey. He has no means of heating his storeroom except the toaster, which he switches on so that we can take turns warming our numb hands over it. Through the window I can see a couple of pheasants pecking along the shining road with all its pointless bends. When I ask him why it is so erratic, he tells me that in the old days the roads had been paved with stones by women who didn't like the wind messing up their hair, so when it changed direction, they did likewise. I find this explanation entirely satisfactory.

The Romans never came here. No Romans, no *urbs*, no milestones, no trace of those systems that reduce nature to straight lines and perpendiculars.

Galway I

There was just a streak of dark saffron in the black sky. I parked the car in between frost-burnt, flattened crocuses. From the terrace you could see the coves north of the port lightly frozen over. It was out of season and this was the only hotel in which I could find a room. Usually it would be closed for the winter, but it had reopened to accommodate young teams of techies from Ireland and the UK who were making a great din. The theme of their meeting, written on posters bordered with mistletoe and holly, was 'Taking our destiny back into our own hands'. There were about a hundred yuppies, but of an Irish kind: built like rugby players, short in the leg, their sideburns ginger or salt-and-pepper, their voices deep and pumiced by Guinness, straight out of an etching from the turn of the century. Their work was at an end and a dinner was to follow. At midday the heating had broken down and despite the lighting of emergency peat fires, which whistled and sighed in the fireplaces, the temperature had continued to fall. The merits of a peat fire are purely visual: its intense redness comforts the eye and fools the body. It burns but gives out no heat; you stretch your hands to the hearth, your shoulders remain frozen while your soles begin to smoke. One after the other, the participants went to the cloakroom in search of mufflers, hats, capes, gloves. Across all this wool, the breath of the last speakers was transformed into misty speech bubbles; they might as well have been sitting outdoors.

It was the only habitable room; I'd been put at a little table in the corner where my dinner was served. When our eyes met, they waved expansively as if I were about to cast off. I understood the closing speeches; the Irish one could be summed up as: 'What a pleasure to be gathered here to drink together.' They didn't stint in filling their shot glasses and despite the Siberian temperature, they remained jovial. The British one could be reduced to: 'It's about time you got down to work.' By the end of the evening, through animal heat and loud talk, the temperature had risen slightly to – let's say – twelve degrees. A few dishevelled women, come from a neighbouring bar to enliven this purely masculine gathering, had kept on their gloves, their scarves and their black straw hats, which gave them the air of decent parishioners, although their faces were turning brick-red and there was nothing but bawdy laughter, tickling and squeezing.

My room was glacial and I called reception. They sent a boy drunk with sleep whom they must have hauled out of bed. He tapped the frozen pipes with his monkey-wrench, saying to himself, 'Guess it must be the pipes' and then, rubbing his eyes, returned to his sleep. He switched off the light as he left; I don't think he'd seen me. I borrowed covers from neighbouring beds and managed to get

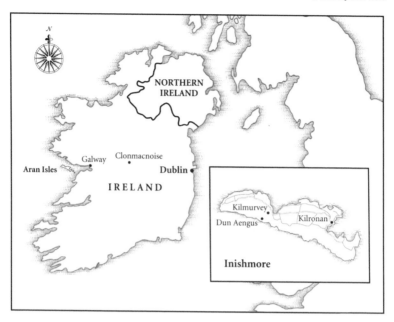

to sleep, only to be woken by an amorous commotion next door: slap and tickle to warm themselves. I heard the woman say in a high-pitched voice: 'No, not that, you're not allowed to...' and I fell back into the dark. Allowed to what? I'm still wondering.

Galway II
11 a.m.
From the cliff-top path, you could see the sparkle on the sea: up to about a hundred metres from the coast it was covered with a thin film of ice, which lifted with the swell like the chest of someone sleeping. A large woman, bulging out of her loud green woollen coat, came up beside me, pushing a pram against the sea breeze which pinned the cold to jaw and temples. Why would you take a nipper for a walk in such weather! She was already big with the next one, and the bruise closing her left eye was no doubt caused by falling against the stove. She told me that she was born here and that she'd never seen the sea frozen like this. The butt stuck to her lower lip trembled with each syllable. Was she thirty, forty? She was already so dog-eared by life that it was difficult to tell. I was just

thinking that despite Synge, Joyce, Shaw and Black Bush whiskey, I would absolutely never be able to settle in a country where the women were dressed any old how – and, moreover, beaten-up – when what I was anxiously waiting for happened: a wave higher than the others, which I had seen out of the corner of my eye, travelled beneath the ice-field and broke it apart. From one end of the bay to the other, it shattered into stars like a car windscreen, with a long sigh, a sort of muffled laugh which startled the seagulls into flight. A photo I had seen twenty years earlier came back to me in a flash. It was of a psychiatrist in a Moravian clinic, who was hypnotising a shawled peasant by tapping his pen against the rim of a crystal glass. I heard the sound of the nib, and saw again the woman in green, moored to her pram like a stone statue, and fell into a 'quasar'...

In the cosmos there are inexplicable black areas that astronomers have dubbed 'quasars'. They are made of such dense matter that photons cannot escape from them – they are the excesses or holes of creation, if you like. In a quasar the mind is undone and retains nothing; before you can take a breath you have already disappeared. You return to the surface somewhere else, a bit later, a bit farther away, in a medium that provides sufficient coherence for you to be able to breathe again. Or you don't return: each year eight thousand people disappear in a puff of smoke without the help of terrorists, an alligator or a disputed will...

... Several hours later, I found myself in the centre of town emerging from a department store with my arms full of purchases: a black-and-white-striped scarf, a red woollen hat and mittens, one of those long, off-white, undergarments, baggy at the knees, seen in etchings by Daumier and farces by Labiche. Exactly what I needed. I looked at the price-tags, the prices were reasonable: in short, the purchases of a man getting on with things. The sky was a dirty pink and black. A sharp, leaden light lent things that were ugly their maximum ugliness, shouting it out. An icy wind swept the narrow street, tearing the red banner saying DOWN WITH APARTHEID IN SOUTH AFRICA! MEETING TONIGHT that a group of young people were engaged on fixing back together to brandish while chanting anti-racist slogans. The passers-by, busy grabbing the last woollens from the stalls, didn't give a tinker's curse. That evening a drop, like a star, hung under every nose. In the St Mary Street market, muffled-up women shut down their stalls, filling boxes with the cabbages, turnips and horseradish they hadn't sold. Coherence? I stamped my feet on the pavement to bring myself back into existence, to reassure myself that I was still here, even if the words *I* and *here* were not quite making sense yet. I had to go all the way round the main square to find my car again, then I took the road to the airport, from which a single engine plane serves the three Aran islands. Wind permitting, it is the only link between the Isles and the coast of Ireland at this season.

Galway III

I was told: 'Leave your car beside the turnip field and give the key to the petrol-pump attendant.' I was told: 'The plane will be delayed, you have plenty of time.' We did have plenty of time. In the sort of caravan which serves as a waiting-room, around a red-hot cast-iron stove, there was a priest armed with the sacraments; a mother with three pale kids each dressed in itchy knee-socks and wine-coloured jackets bought in the Galway sales, who scratched their calves in that sly and stubborn way that little girls often have; an old lady, her white hair in a neat bun, holding on her lap a rush basket exactly tailored to the shape of a hen with a hole for its neck and head, which were sticking out of it and, beak open, were surveying the tiny room with a panic-stricken movement; a young madam in stunningly elegant boots who was reading Orwell's *1984* – just one year late – not looking at anyone, turning the pages with perfectly shaped, oval, gilded nails; a ewe whose back left leg had just been put in plaster by the vet on the mainland, and who would be travelling in the hold; and lastly the pilot, very reassuring in his crumpled uniform, who had weighed each passenger as though we were there for a weight-loss clinic. Then there was the blessed roar of the engine over the sea, which was turning black. We landed at Inishmaan in a barely marked field, time to deposit the priest, his oil-can and some parcels tied with stout string, and then were off again without cutting the engine for the 'Big Island' (Inishmore), a flight which must be the shortest in the tables of commercial aviation, that is, three minutes forty-five seconds.

Aran I

Five minutes this time; the plane had regained a little altitude; time enough for a yellow Land Rover to disperse the grazing sheep with a virtuoso slalom and to arrive beside the cabin, ready to lift off the bags and convey each passenger to their destination. Michael Hernon, the driver, was a man in his forties, laconic, polite, precise, reserved, with the patina of old driftwood that you often find in windswept lands. I helped him carry the ewe in plaster as far as the peristyle of a dark house. The beauty – I had thought she would accompany the priest to the bedside of the dying man – was the hairdresser at Kilronan and puffed out or slicked down every head of hair in the archipelago. We deposited her in front of a dry-stone cottage; its one windowless wall displayed a fresco of the two special house-styles: the Teddy Boy cut, and the 1930s' Marcel Wave which was back in fashion, although it may never have been out of it here. In Killeany Bay, the west wind which swirled round the island whisked up little waterspouts which skittered off in the direction of Galway. I was the last passenger. I asked Hernon what people did here at this time of year.

'After the January storms, if the west wind sets in, they do nothing. The waves are too strong for coastal fishing. The trawlermen go off to Norway and are away for a fortnight or so. They take the fish that's already frozen to Galway, and when they come back, everything that has no commercial use – octopus, skate, spotted dogfish, eel – they give away.'

'They don't sell them?'

'They keep what they need, then give the rest to the village; there's enough for everyone, they all come and help themselves.'

'And the fields?'

'The walls around the kitchen gardens get repaired but the wind's too strong to spread seaweed on the meadows, it blows over the stone walls and then you have to start all over again. The men do odd jobs around the house, and drink; the women knit for the summer tourist trade. And not just any old knitting: each of the island villages, even if there are only four or five houses, has its pattern, like a brand. In the old days it was a way to identify the drowned who washed up on shore: crabs and fish don't eat wool. Today it's only the drunk who drown; they have their separate corner in the cemetery.'

He stopped at the edge of the hamlet of Kilmurvey, in front of the only lighted house for several leagues around.

'Here we are; they're expecting you. I'll come and get you tomorrow and take you to the foot of the western cliffs – if you aren't afraid of the spray or heights.'

I'm not afraid of heights. We'll see how it goes.

Aran II

I knocked and went in: there was one huge room running the length of the façade. At each end a fire hissed and glowed, burning a mixture of peat and coal. On the left-hand side, seated in front of the fire in a raspberry-velvet armchair, an old man with a fine-featured, waxen face drew on his pipe. He welcomed me with a touch of his hand to the brim of his tweed cap, which I never saw him without. It was the uncle. While a black dog and a white dog nuzzled my legs, the nephew came out of the kitchen, tea-towel in hand. Steve: in his fifties, stocky, with luxuriant whiskers, and the lively and alert air of one who's been around; an incisor missing from his upper jaw gave him the look of an extremely wary rabbit. The upstairs room was small, monastic, perfect: a black iron bedstead with a gilded rose at the head and foot; a plump blue quilt; a white china washbasin patterned with clematis; a little wardrobe. In my bag, a small bottle of excellent whiskey which must have been one of my Galway purchases. The three of us sipped it as we became acquainted.

Like many islanders, the uncle had feathered his nest in America in a variety of jobs. For years he had been a stoker on the tugboats which pulled rafts of logs across Lake Michigan. The arrival of the Great Depression found him stoking the boilers of a huge laundry, run by Irish nuns, where they sterilised tons of verminous rags belonging to the derelict and unemployed in the Bronx. Despite the stifling atmosphere of the boiler-room and the pittance he earned, he had liked the work: to exterminate millions of lice, nits and domestic bugs (*cimex lectularius*) had seemed to him a sort of crusade.

'Each time I shovelled a load of coal, I'd see a whole street stop scratching.'

Through who knows what patronage, this scourge of lice then passed seamlessly to the cloakroom of the Algonquin Hotel, from stinking rags to the vicuna and blue fox of stars and gangsters. In helping people on with their coats, the natural distinction of this ex-boilerman had worked wonders in that world of operatic, generous upstarts. He had summoned his nephew to help him run this deluxe wardrobe where no one disputed his rule. At the beginning of the 1970s they had returned to their own country, their pockets full. They were made much of: they were bringing in money and above all fresh news; there was quite a colony of islanders in New York and on Aran they felt closer to Brooklyn than to Dublin. What's more, no one was jealous of success because everyone here hoped for it – or had succeeded – just as much. The nephew had built this large cottage just as tourism was taking off. In the high season, he accommodates and feeds a dozen or so guests who all become friends. He likes cooking for them, drinking with them, asking them questions.

'For thirty years I was always coming and going, moving from one job to another in America, and now the world comes to me: the Dutch, Swedes, Italians, Americans. Bird-watchers, botanists, linguists, philosophers. From May to September there isn't a free night.'

The uncle who had given him a leg up and was the source of his success would live in comfort for the rest of his days. He looks after the kitchen garden, some dahlias, walks the dogs, seasons his pipe, and spends at least half his time with his memories. When he remembers aloud, it's good to be within earshot. The two of them make a perfect team, like the fox and the wolf in the old tale. With one difference, the fact that they inhabit separate worlds, so that a stranger like me must talk to them separately in terms of content and form: the uncle believes in spirits, the nephew does not.

The uncle said to me: 'If you go for a walk, take the black dog with you. He's called Alabar; there's no risk of his getting run over here.'

The nephew said to me: 'What an idea to come here at the height of the winter storms! At the end of May we have thirty-five varieties of orchid and wild anemones and nineteen kinds of bee. And now: nothing, nothing at all. We eat at eight, does that suit you?' That suited me. And the idea of landing up here wasn't mine.

Nothing is a specious word which conveys nothing. *Nothing* always sets me thinking. It is not that the forecast puts these islands under narcosis, that they cease to exist. Inishmore is still there on the map, with its eight hundred inhabitants, even if they lie low like lobsters in their cottages to struggle against the depression which seizes you after several days of continual wind.

Padded like an Eskimo, I went out to see what this nothing was made of. The night rose from the ground like an inky blanket, no light, the black of the walls even darker than the black of the fields. A howling gale; my fists froze in the depths of my pockets. Alabar didn't follow me for long: this nothing said nothing worthwhile to him. He turned round and scratched at the door which was soon opened. I was looking for the hermitage of St Enda, the one whose disciples had founded the monastery of St Gall and taught the rustics that we were how to cross ourselves, say grace, sing plainsong and illuminate manuscripts with ornate capitals, teeming with interlaced griffins, hawthorn, unicorns. According to my map, his den should be just two hundred metres east of the house. Obviously I didn't find it that evening – by day it turned out to be a low, mossy molehill, so basic that beside it the shepherds' huts in Gordes look like the Facteur Cheval's palace.* But I did see – my eyes becoming accustomed to the night – a pale shape, huddled in the angle formed by two low walls. It was a white carthorse, so huge and still that at first I thought it was a gigantic effigy left behind by some Atlantis, unknown to archaeologists, which the winter winds had stripped of its lichen and barnacles and polished to this opaline perfection. He had found the most sheltered corner and, his muzzle stuck to his breast, he was staying put, so as to be less cold. Without the shiver that ran from tail to nostrils, I would have sworn he was made of plaster. What an idea to leave a horse alone in the icy wind without even a mare to warm him! And what an idea blindly to seek the hermitage of a saint dead these fourteen centuries, stepping across low dry-stone walls, knocking down stones that I had to put back in place. I was trying to tiptoe across the horse's patch without attracting his attention when I heard a heavy tread and was practically lifted off the ground as he shoved his nose under

---

* The Facteur (Ferdinand) Cheval (1836–1924) was a French postman who spent decades building his extraordinarily ornate *Palais Idéal* out of stones in Hauterives, south-eastern France. (Translator's note)

my arms; with pasterns the size of beehives and his huge, insistent presence, muzzle rooting in the warmth like a snout, he propelled me like a wisp of straw as far as the road, leaving shining traces of snot which I have only just finished removing from the back of my coat. There was no way of warding him off with a sign of the cross or a druidic sprinkler. He took me as far as the wall bordering the road, tossed me there like a cloth by butting me with his head, then returned to his business. And I to mine, first of all to finding my lodging; in passing from one plot of land to the next, I had lost my way. The night was now so dark that only the sharper sound made by my boots told me that I was back on the road. A few metres from the house, two blazing gold eyes which pierced the blackness at about waist height made me turn round: they belonged to a tomcat, as white and, for his breed, as large as the horse, huddled beside a low wall. His body exactly filled the sides of a hole left by a stone that the wind (or he himself) had dislodged. The only thing sticking out were his whiskers, where a scrap of cod was caught, and tonight wasn't the night to turn him out of his cell. The frown on his face suggested only resentment and spite. What on earth was he doing outdoors in these high winds when in the cottages barricaded behind their drawn shutters and deceptive darkness there was – I knew – a hearth where peat-smoke twisted, a lighted corner where women plied their needles and kids stuck out their tongues in concentration as they wrote their homework with steel-nibbed pens that caught and scratched? A stallion: that's one thing. I could understand that a horse by the fireside, especially the size of the one that had just left me – however good-natured he might be – posed a volumetric problem that even a student who was good at his homework could not easily solve. But a cat? Had he been caught in the act of stealing dried fish and flung out of doors? I'd have to find out.

I ate with my hosts and drank some of the excellent Chianti given to them by an Italian television crew they had put up last summer during a shoot. Over the rim of their glasses, they cautiously examined me; I felt that my presence here, at this season, disconcerted them. They didn't see strangers on the islands in winter, apart from the occasional horse-dealer from Galway, or a gypsy who discovers and undoes the evil eye, or a small-scale shipowner on the coast come to negotiate the price of a tuna-boat. That a journalist, especially a photographer, should choose the worst time of the year (I had chosen nothing: I had been sent) to make a visit seemed suspicious to them. They scented a scam. The previous year, property developers had come to the island in the guise of tourists, had been found out and escorted politely back to their boat.

I showed them an example of the magazine for which I worked, but this only seemed to increase their puzzlement and, perhaps, their frustration. It was an issue about Rajasthan, where the saris and the ornate façades the colours of sorbet, vibrant in the dusk, gleamed and literally swallowed up the pages. Here, there was no colour other than the grey of the horizon and the low stone walls and the green algae on the stubble fields. A strict duotone, washed rather than enlivened by the pale disc of the sun, which the swift, eastward-running clouds obscured more often than unveiled. For a week no one here would cast a shadow. Seven years earlier, I had toured the island in May. Fine. It was a hundred times more beautiful in the sheer wildness of the winter storms.

Under my window the neighbour's sheep shivered side by side, making the fence round their enclosure shake, and it sang in the wind like a ship's rigging. With their matchstick legs and tightly curled fleeces they reminded me of a drawing by a child of the Viennese decadence: the unhealthy, emaciated bodies of Egon Schiele drowning in Sacher-Masoch's furs.

The nephew came grumbling upstairs: 'A hundred and thirty-five kinds of flower and nineteen kinds of bee.' By coming out of season, I had caught him at a disadvantage. He knew how to boast about his brimstone anemones, he had not yet learnt to sell the wind. It didn't matter: I love storms, and the North, and the winter.

Nothing? Yet a stallion, a tomcat, sheep, this bestiary shivering in the polar cold and this continual roaring – they weren't nothing. Rather, they were 'something else'. I wasn't slow to join in the general trembling, however: having slipped under my enormous quilt, I could still hear a heartrending bleating, and my teeth began to chatter with the onset of a fever, just what's wanted where there isn't a doctor. Who knew which little cousin of those young ladies on the big island last week had landed me with the paratyphoid which was about to melt me like lard in a frying pan.

Kilmurvey, Inishmore, Aran
17 February

When Edmund Ross observed the Eskimos of Baffin Bay during his second Arctic voyage in 1832, he recorded that the thermal equilibrium of an igloo was such that a single whale-oil lamp gave out sufficient heat for the women, seated on a bench of ice, to strip to the waist. The expedition's artist has left us a beautiful lithograph of one of these charmers, with thick, oiled plaits and breasts like mortar shells. Another image entitled 'First Encounter' shows Eskimos running across an ice-floe to meet Ross in his cocked hat with its gold braid, their arms lifted in a sign of welcome as though to meet Father Christmas. Ross has his hand on the pommel of his sword, with the air of a man who isn't certain how things will turn out. They turned out very well, and the Eskimos soon revealed themselves as virtuoso cuckolds, for a small return palming off the wives for whom they no longer had any use to those Englishmen deprived of women. Ross, who considered them to be as intelligent as they were adaptable, must have wondered why such an industrious people – they were not yet undermined by alcohol – hadn't moved farther south to settle in a milder climate.

Similarly, no history of Ireland explains what led the Celts, several centuries before Christ, to settle on these outer, windswept islands, separated by dangerous seas, which appeared as huge slabs of bare rock gently sloping from western cliffs to sheltered inlets facing Galway Bay. The huge dry-stone amphitheatres found here, built well before the Christian era and described – wrongly – as forts (*dun* in Gaelic), suggest a population almost as large as today's. So why? Flight from a rival, conquering clan? A sea rich in fish that offered refuge and a livelihood to incomparably skilful sailors and fishermen? No one knows. And when did the Sisyphean labour begin, transforming the rock into vegetable gardens and pasture for sheep? It can't be dated, but to judge by the method of fertilising these stony acres, still in use in the 1930s, it must have begun a very long time ago, perhaps as far back as the early Middle Ages when Ireland was still a breeding-ground for wild energy and daredevil dynamism. They attacked the rock with wedges and sledgehammers to dig out deep parallel furrows, half a metre wide. With chunks of the broken stone they created a low wall which marked the boundary of the rockery of which they were – all too often – only tenants. Then they filled the trenches with a mixture of fine sand and kelp, which men and women would cut at low tide and carry up from the beach in rush creels. After this mixture was laid down, they would plant a few potatoes or a bit of rye to maintain their thatched roofs. One or two years later, they destroyed the ridges of stone between the trenches and raised and reinforced the walls with the cleared material, strewing the enclosed surface with successive layers of seaweed which, over time, produced plots of good arable land. Not that they owned this land themselves: at the beginning of this century, most of the island was still in outsiders' hands. It only took one bad year, one late rental for the proprietor (Irish or English landowner) to take over and expel the islander from the plot that had quintupled in value. That was when the constable, accompanied by a stinking bailiff in his black suit, would help himself to a pig, a heifer, a crib of plaited willow, a cooking-pot, a woollen shawl... These evictions were as brutal as those which, a bit earlier, had darkened Scotland. Sometimes the bedridden were turned out in their beds, in the rain, while the police ransacked the cottage, and the old women of the hamlet – a sort of coven – would surround the evildoers with shrill curses which the clergy, foolishly smug, believed they had robbed of all potency. I am willing to bet that not a week went by without one of those guardians of order – cop or notary – kicking the bucket, carried off by a form of epilepsy unknown to medical students.

Today, everything on the rock that could be taken back has been; basically the island belongs to those who, at the price of inconceivable labour, have turned this grey rock into fresh green, have transformed it into a paradise for botanists and ornithologists. When you look down from the height of the western cliffs and see the network of low walls – twelve thousand kilometres from end to end – which covers the island and seems to hold it in a net of tight stitches, and when you consider the rustic nature of the techniques used, all the things the Irish say complacently about their own laziness and their incurable dreaminess seem so much nonsense. It is true that those same Irishmen laughingly claim to be the best liars on the Atlantic coast, and they are right about that.

So It Goes

The same morning

From the toilet seat to which persistent dysentery had pinned me for half the night, I saw through the skylight the day dawning over the dulled fields, the maze of grey walls, the bronzed steel of the sea. In the big room downstairs, the fires were out. Drinking a cup of scalding tea, almost solid with sugar, I could hear the fever racing through me, while asking myself what I could learn from this 'lesson in less'. At nine o'clock, Michael and his yellow Land Rover were in the courtyard. There was no question of going along the reef-like rocks beneath the western cliffs. There was too much wind for the lengthy approach, which you could only make on foot. Off we went towards the north-westernmost point of the island, bumping along a road with enormous potholes, which ended without warning beside a lagoon of still water. There were three coracles there – *curraghs*, the canoes the islanders use for coastal fishing – turned over, fastened with ropes, waiting for the summer months to be caulked and returned to the water, and a great jumble of rubbish and drifting debris which circled the island according to the gales and tides. Two black swans as well, the Australian variety, drawn from a store of Wagnerian accessories, sleeping afloat, totally unconcerned. Glacial cold. Swift grey clouds blotted out the light. To the north, not far away, the two small isles of Brannock, uninhabited in this season. Indescribably desolate. Michael got out of the car, struggling with the door which the wind tore from his hand. He had – I hadn't noticed the previous evening – a built-up shoe and a limp, no doubt the after-effects of polio. Standing on the shore, shading his eyes, and with his back turned towards Europe, looking westwards where the sea boiled and bubbled like a cauldron, he said to me with dry satisfaction: 'Next bus-stop, New York…' Then the wind freshened and made any conversation impossible. Beyond being there, we had nothing to say to each other anyway. Wild rabbits, their little white scuts trembling, popped up and disappeared beneath our feet. This shore was one of those non-places which travelling keeps up its sleeve for us. I had known others, and I felt fine there.

On the road back, we came across a cart and bolting horse. Michael mounted the verge to let it pass. The large, red-haired driver of this outfit, which was heading disastrously for the beach, was bent double over the reins but, despite the urgency of his situation, let go with one hand to wave at us before disappearing in an ominous cloud of dust.

Whether you are on foot, in a car, on horseback or in flight, it is unimaginable to cross someone's path here without greeting them. On the island, everyone knows everyone else, but men also touched a finger to their hat brim to welcome a stranger such as myself. Michael told me that no one was in difficulties here if they needed a hand. He thought that this solidarity – both cheerful and taciturn – was due to the precariousness of island existence for so many years. The harder and more frugal life is, the better those Gaelic blessings ('a hundred thousand welcomes', or 'many happy returns') ameliorate and ease it. There are no great social differences on the island. Some people – my hosts – are better off than others, but the poverty of the old days has gone. Neither nouveaux riches nor shame-faced poor. Few are envious. They are very aware of the advantages of this balance here, and oppose anything that might compromise it. A week before my arrival, people from Aran had massed in Galway, invoking a right of pre-emption to buy back a large plot of land which was up for sale, and to prevent the construction of a tourist complex which would have strangled trade for the families who provide home-stays for visitors in the summer on terms which no hotelier could boast of providing. It is a very personalised hospitality. People talk, they write to each other, they connect and they return. They pay, too, and more than compensate for the loss from fishing, where for several years prices have dropped and the cost of fuel has shaved off the profits. Besides, these summer friends bring news of the world which sharpens, if it were needed, the natural curiosity of the Aran islanders.

Everywhere tourism is slammed: it's fashionable to do it, it's in good taste, and often justifiable. In many cases it is a demeaning relationship, both for the tourists and for the people who, in their big clogs that you hear clattering a mile away, try and always succeed in ripping them off. A rotten affair based on mutual misunderstanding. Most of the countries living off it haven't really accepted it; as soon as they are among their own kind, they make fun of the foreigner they've cheated. But not here: it's too small, too distinctive, too far away; the sea is too cold or too strong. The stranger is considered a godsend and, above all, like a Mercury who can be questioned with discreet persistence. Godsends screened by some method which escapes me: in my hosts' stories I never encountered anyone pretentious, any rednecks or hooligans. And in their golden book were: a philologist from Berlin (the Gaelic spoken here is said to be the best in Ireland); a Dutch couple, ornithologists; farmers from the American corn-belt in search of their origins and, perhaps, a grave; English people charmed by the changing light which would have been irresistible to Turner; a whole pack of theosophical-macrobiotic Danish teachers with perfect complexions and plump knees, who gathered scabious for their herbarium, painted watercolours, went cycling, and whom the island's rugged widowers, leaning against the white walls of their cottages, watched with a dreamy gaze as they passed, who filled plastic bags full of the rubbish that the islanders – however fussy they were about the cleanliness of their cottages – dropped anywhere, and sent such staunchly Polar Christmas cards that they made everyone feel a citizen of the world. The people here are proud of the island which they have literally made with their own hands, its excellence beyond question. That people should come from far away to visit it – what could be more natural? Money? Of course it plays a part, but the prices are reasonable and they have too much self-respect to swindle the customer. As it declares in letters of gold gleaming against a shamrock-green background in the only pub in Kilronan: INCOME IS NOT EVERYTHING.

That evening
'Feed a cold, starve a fever.' The nephew isn't happy because I turn up my nose at his excellent cooking, but my gums are too swollen and sore to do it justice. I starve my fever at the fireside, drinking tea and listening to the uncle. I don't recall having asked him a single question. It's enough for me to sit down opposite him, and tap my spoon against the cup, for his stories to start to sing softly like a kettle over the fire. Even if I weren't there he would tell these things over again to himself. I am there, and he fills the emptiness of this island, which the wind has snuffed out like a candle, with his stories. Moreover, he speaks the handsome American of the forties, of Raymond Chandler, Dashiell Hammett, Lauren Bacall, of the

fantastic Algonquin cloakroom, with its mix of stars and mafiosi, to which he had summoned his nephew and where fortune had smiled on them. From Fred Astaire to Greta Garbo, Bette Davis to Gene Kelly to the *Cosa Nostra* godfathers – it was about who had shown themselves the most generous. At Christmas 1950, they had made ten thousand dollars in tips between the two of them, living the American dream. Then *Goodbye, Manhattan*. Was he bored? At first, yes: strings of pearls, satin skin, gleaming fedoras, heaving or withered breasts, voices gravelly or crystalline, this dance of thieves in fine linen – with his natural shrewdness, he knew perfectly well that he missed their magic. And New York was full of Irish living much better than in their own country. On his return, he had also found things greatly changed.

'When I left, the priest said mass with his face to the altar and you opened your mouth for the Host. It's not like that now. It doesn't matter; what counts is that life has become better here.'

The uncle, who goes willingly to church, had never had any faith in anything the priest might say.

'Always the same. He only talked about damnation, not about us. If you so much as messed up a girl's hair, you would go straight as an arrow to hell.'

He didn't believe in all of that. He believed in 'places' (the Breton word is *ker*). He knew particular places on the island – a rock split by lightning, the clump of dogwood which had always been there and refused to die – which were full of efficacious power and goodness. That was where you had to go to meditate, pray, give thanks. Elsewhere, as in the church which was rather left to the women, it was a waste of time. He didn't tell me where or how to find them: it's up to each of us to discover them and know what they want from us. They don't draw attention to themselves but lie hidden with their freight of gifts or threats. If you approach them from the left or the right your day will be different. Here, folk have so long been accustomed to such ancient magic that it has become almost benign and homely, while still keeping its place. The clergy, who have always been afraid of nature – at the trial of Joan of Arc it was held against her that she danced beneath an oak tree on the feast of St John – are theatrical figures with their superfluous props and posturing. They aren't taken as seriously as I had feared.

Sometimes the uncle would interrupt his tale to put his hand over his mouth and burp discreetly. At others he would fall asleep on the spot in his armchair, and his cap would descend a notch over his eyes. I would then go and lie down, or rather, shiver between the bed and the bathroom. The uncle was a light sleeper, and although I tried to be as quiet as a mouse, he heard me go to and fro half the night with my muffled tread. This gave him something to think about. He treated me with that mixture of suspicion and complicity reserved for those whose identity is not well established.

Kilmurvey, 18 February, morning
Some days, one would gladly do without a body; colic and fever allow me four hours of sleep, a welcome respite before dawn which I use to separate myself from it. On waking, I find it again at arms' length. I rub it down, I attack it with cold water and a brush, I rub it with camphor-oil; I simply send it back and am amused to find it again each morning a bit thinner and more pathetic. I wrap it in wool and leather, make it swallow very sweet tea – the only food it can take – then send it out on the road where it is fed by the Atlantic winds and where I join it a little later without having spoken a word to it. However awful the night, a few gulps of air are enough to steady it. There it is, reinvigorated, quite ready for what the day might hold.

I remember that in Macedonia you could not stop at a village, even the poorest, without someone saying, 'Ah, you've come to taste our water,' each one claiming a better spring than the neighbours'. With anxious attention they watched you drinking the misted glass they had offered, as if it were a great vintage, and your noisy gulping and compliments would indicate how many gold stars you would award it.

In such a game, the Aran air would win any competition. All the good things I could say about what one breathes here, in this raging weather, with its scent of wild fennel and the vapour of sea-water, would not come near the truth. It expands, invigorates, intoxicates, lightens, sets free those animal spirits in the head which have us surrendering to unknown, hilarious games. It unites the virtues of champagne, cocaine, caffeine and the ecstasy of love, and the tourist office is quite wrong to leave it out of its brochures. In India, I had seen 'pneumatic' gurus tuck away litres of air in their stomachs, then release the air, in the process munching up all its nutritional elements like pancakes straight from the oven. Without making any effort. Here I lived well on it for a week of strict fasting and tiring walks in a sort of stunned intoxication.

With Michael I climbed as far as the village of Gortnagapple: three cottages without any smoke surrounded by tufts of willow-herb browned by the winter. From there, walking westwards downhill, you reach a saddle where the cliff is eaten away and crumbling into huge boulders which the winter storms push farther inland each year. Blocks weighing several tons have been rolled into fields like single dice in a poker game. Once you have crossed this chaos, you reach a vast chalk terrace, battered by the sea, slippery with seaweed, holed like cheese, starred with lichen ranging from ox-blood red to Memling green, shining in the brief moments the sea retreats – we seize on those in order to leap across the crevices in which it thunders like a bombardment. Michael goes in front, to show me the way, more agile than a troll despite his boot. Faces reddened, hair stuck down with brine and sea-spray, we have the greatest difficulty in remaining upright. I was wondering what could justify such a risky route when we arrive above a pool that is an absolutely symmetrical rectangle. The sea which rushed beneath this terrace had split it apart and given to this cavity such a perfect shape – sharp angles and edges as if drawn with precision and a plumb line – that it is impossible not to imagine plans, stonecutters, human labour, albeit this magic cauldron has absolutely no purpose. This natural phenomenon is all the more intriguing in that, apart from being found in certain forms of crystal and blood platelets, the rectangle is a very rare shape in the animal, vegetable or mineral realm, so this instance has given rise to the most fantastic theories. It has been claimed that the pool is the cusp of a tunnel that, in the golden age of Atlantis, linked the island to the Connemara coast, but the divers who have explored it in periods of calm have not found anything to support such nonsense. As neither historians nor geologists offer a valid explanation of this enigma, it is more reasonable to think that when nature – which does not ask for our opinion – wishes to offer up a perfect rectangle, it does so without stinting.

I left Michael in the grip of a peasant who had come up from the shore with a barrow-load of kelp. They were speaking Gaelic; I only knew that it concerned the price of a calf. I climbed by myself, zigzagging between gentians and low walls, as far as the fort of Dun Aengus, which crowns the highest cliff. I heard the sea battering its foot without seeing it, aware the wrathful wind was coming head on and looking for a way round. I said to myself, 'all the same… in a hundred metres', and believed I would be under cover. I was wrong. A wind which had picked up from Newfoundland would not let itself be fooled by a cliff, however imposing. For the wind it was less an obstacle than a riddle to which it had long known the answer. This is how it works: at the foot of the cliff it forms a cushion of air; from this springboard it rises up and starts again. When, having made the climb, it reaches the top and hurtles down the other slope in almighty gusts which flatten broom and thistles, it is better not to stand in its way. A few metres from the fort, one of these gusts hit me, throwing me to the ground and tossing me into the stones and brambles like yesterday's newspaper. I saw my heavy camera bag bounding ahead to the green meadows, scattering the rabbits, and found shelter in a corner of the fort, hands and nose bleeding from scratches. A petrel, wounded by the wind which had hurled it like a stone against the cliff, circled round me, limping. I lit a cigarette and began to laugh. I had always chafed at my heaviness; to be tossed about like a fallen leaf had made my blood tingle. For the first time since I'd been here, I glimpsed the sun through a momentary parting of the dirty clouds. It showed itself for fifteen or sixteen seconds, long enough to photograph my shadow as proof of my having been there. As for the rest…

Dun Aengus

You will find several of these curious dry-stone constructions on the west coast and the islands. Dun Aengus is the most important. It is a semicircle which rises in tiers around a platform where the rock has been levelled precisely to the edge of the cliff – a vertiginous drop. The *cheval de frise* of upright limestone shards preventing access endorses the thesis that this was a military site. *Dun* in Gaelic means 'fortress'. Yet this seems absurd: someone inside would be able to see nothing at all of what might be plotted outside. No arrow-slits, no crenellations for surveillance of the surroundings. Silently scaling the outside wall would be a child's game, the other being to hurl the defenders taken by surprise into the void. Instead, I imagine it was an amphitheatre for solemn ceremonies, enthronements, seasonal rituals, or for druid assemblies where the plunge of the sun into the sea was accompanied by a chorus of lamentation. Scholarly works make assertions as durable as myths, and they insist on describing these constructions as 'forts'. A Galway professor shares my doubts, but when I consulted him on this matter, he simply replied that it took a long time to get something into an Irish head, and therefore it would need an even longer time to dislodge it.

I paused there to listen to the battering sea, to hear the wind as it snatched like a thief at its misty covers, braying in my face, then I dawdled down to the eastern coves. On Kilmurvey Bay, in the patches sheltered by low stone walls, migratory birds had come crashing down in their hundreds, with a deafening chirping; clad in shining black with white fronts and bottle-green crests, they were a little bit smaller than European hoopoes.

Kilmurvey, late afternoon
The uncle had also seen these migrants. It had been forty years since they had last been to the island. It was the cold front that had brought them here. Together we found out what they were, in an ornithological guide donated by a summer guest: Siberian blackbirds. During their last visit – when the island was poorer – he had plucked a few for spit-roasting: too tough to be eaten.

Later
At the fireside, empty-headed, buzzing with fatigue, I dab my scratches with iodine. Deep inside, somewhere, I feel that life goes on in perfect freedom, circulates, breaks up and rolls on like drops of mercury. I suspect that ideas pay a visit, that concepts challenge and amuse themselves without inviting me. These games are beyond my reach, although I hear their faint sound. Servant and doorman to myself, once again I find myself shut out.

So It Goes

I came here with only one book. Deliberately. The sense of destitution, emptiness, nothingness born from this deprivation is no surprise; it is a healthy exercise. When this central vacuum, which I have covered over or filled with empty distractions somehow or other, becomes unbearable, I know that I must hold on to it, wait for a lock to spring, for an unknown gate in me to open on a moment of liberty as fresh as a bunch of watercress. Patience. Physical exhaustion – I walked all day with no feeling in my legs – gives another chance for these attempts at evasion or invasion.

The one book is an anthology of Celtic sagas in their oldest form. It has just dropped from my hands. Betrayals through ambushes, promises made in oaths that were broken, complicated plots – I lose the thread of the story and lose interest in the way that these wily folk killed each other. Moreover, there are so many sudden metamorphoses, and identities are so changeable, that I never know who is doing what: whether the dragonfly is a princess, whether the princess is a heavenly mare with whom the mad, red-haired chief of the clan must enter into a mystical union in a huge cauldron. You have seen an apple: it's a witch, red with the sins she is about to commit. It's all too much. I suspect that the monks who copied out these tales deliberately peppered them with misunderstandings and plot twists which mislead and tire us in order to lessen the power they had over naïve souls… and the fashionable Celticisers then followed by adding so many asterisks and footnotes that they killed off what remained of the taste of the broth. The Irish are the first to claim that their history is made up of recantations and sly tricks, which I only half-believe.

'Ugh!' (The uncle who had been sleeping woke up.)

'? ! ?'

'I was dreaming of those birds you reminded me about. The smell of mud.'

Kilmurvey, 19 February, morning

A gorgeous, tall woman, in boots and sou'wester, blue-eyed and raven-haired, has arrived in her van to deliver the coal they mix with the peat for fires. She would be better suited to the upper deck of a privateer. I hear her bantering with the nephew in the kitchen: laughter, sounds of slamming, laughter. She is still laughing and tossing her magnificent head of hair as she drives away. When he comes back in, I compliment him on his beautiful coalwoman; he looks at me with the happy smile of a man who's been given more than he expected. For a moment, we become lads again.

This interlude of spring flirtation made me all the happier because it was less than seventeen degrees fahrenheit in the courtyard, and because the islanders, in this respect, are extremely reserved – although it goes with their natural dignity.

Here, women are treated with the respect that their ingenuity – they turn their hands to anything – their endurance and their courage deserve. Until the 1960s, everyone's lives were too hard anyway to leave much room for romance and libido. Even today, according to Michael, most girls are virgins when they marry, scandal is very rare and crimes of passion are left to the big cities. Besides, there is nothing like a prison on the islands, except at the coastguards' office where there is a room that can be locked, to protect a drunk when he's plastered. This restraint is not due to the influence of the dog-collar, which is minimal here, but to the power of the family unit without which, for a long while, people wouldn't have survived.

Nevertheless, there's a need to confess misdemeanours sometimes, and the priests are on the lookout for rewardingly juicy details. The proverbial prying of the clergy (the confession manuals in which each caress or perversion has its exact penitence tariff are a hundred times more obscene than the eroticism of Hindu temples) is met with local terseness and Anglo-Saxon understatement. They tell here of a priest pressing for details of the frolics during a night spent with a 'friend', to which his parishioner replied: 'I think I remember having dozed off for a bit.'

Later

The Irish of the 'Pale' – the eastern counties north of Dublin and Dundalk – were exposed to invasion, occupation and the successive influence of Norsemen, Normans and English, which created a rich cultural compost, hybrid and ambiguous. For a long time the West was regarded as consisting of nothing but peat, storms, patois and sheep, and its inhabitants as rough-hewn country bumpkins. At the time of the Irish Revival, towards the end of the nineteenth century, it was towards this 'Bogland' (the peat country, but also in the pejorative sense of godforsaken) that certain intellectuals turned, troubled about their identity. Not all of them: it was the beginning of a controversial squabble, typically Irish. Yeats sent Synge to the Aran Isles so that he could learn Gaelic; Joyce wouldn't go there for anything in the world, regarding this return to origins as fraudulent and retrograde, a matter for mockery. Here, no one bothered to hold such fixed opinions: there was no time for them. Dublin? The derby, the races: there is interest in those, but its mayor is less well known here than the mayor of New York. If there is a touch of insular chauvinism, I never found a trace of cultural chauvinism: no question of deafening themselves with ballads, bards or bagpipes. Nor of fighting for a nostalgic Gaeldom, because it's on hand daily, without having to get it down from the shelf or be nostalgic about it. The Celtic crusade was above all a matter for urban intellectuals. Synge returned to the Aran islands four years in a row and devoted a book to them, famous these days, to which the islanders refer from time to time with a typically distant interest. What he could tell them about themselves mattered less than what he could tell them of the world beyond themselves. He could not disembark without hearing, after a greeting: 'Noble stranger, is there a war going on somewhere in the world at present?' The last they'd had wind of was that in the Philippines, which had ended two or three years earlier.*

The people of Aran do not make a great deal of their saints, even though they brought Christianity to half of Europe. I am tempted to believe that they have more or less forgotten them.

Kilronan, Saturday morning
The primitive monasticism of the West of Ireland was so nourished by the wild forces (witchcraft or weather, one and the same) which it had to fight and curb that, for the established Church, it always

---

* What J. M. Synge wrote in *The Aran Islands* (published in 1907) was: 'Noble stranger, is there any great wonder out in the world at this time?' He doesn't actually mention war in that sentence, although he remarks that war is one of their favourite topics: 'Of all the subjects we can talk of war seems their favourite, and the conflict between America and Spain is causing a great deal of excitement.' That was the ten-week war between the two countries in 1898, fought in the Caribbean and the Pacific. (Trs.)

smacked of heresy. At the Council of Valence (in the ninth century) it was already being condemned for 'devilries', and right up to the nineteenth century, Rome never stopped seeing the Irish church as an *enfant terrible* and calling it to order. Over time it lost much of its provocative antagonism and was tamed. Yet in American films and thrillers of the 1950s, one finds pugnacious, daredevil Irish priests who are worthy successors of St Patrick or St Columbanus.

On the islands the church is far from holding sway; rather, it has had to hybridise and enrich itself by incorporating all the beliefs and practices that preceded it. The pledges made by the Church? The protection of the Virgin Mary? Good… plus the fairies, wizards, a dozen kinds of trolls and some stumps inhabited by spirits… even better. But this other-world is also doomed to disappear, along with those who still believe in it.

The grocery store at the port, where I wanted to buy pens, paper and tobacco, is closed. The church is open, a wedding party coming out: new tweed suits shining in the frost, faces red with excitement. The parish priest, a beefy man with frizzy hair, is frenetically dispensing thumps, handshakes, embraces, slaps on the back. He is doing too much of this forced familiarity, perhaps because of the cold. He hasn't the look of a saintly man or even a wise one – more like a rugby coach after a converted try.

Kilronan pub, late afternoon
The pub, also closed because of the wind, has just reopened, in time to cater for those left behind by the wedding, too old or too poor to whoop it up in a hotel in Galway, a celebration that would last at least two days: four men of indeterminate age in caps or woollen balaclavas who don't reply to my greeting. They are at the bar to drink bitter, as silent and motionless as wax statues. If they stir, it's only a forearm, to lift the tankard to their lips; if they drone a few words, it's beneath their breath and without looking at each other. It's as though they have all suddenly received the same bad news without having dared to look at it yet. This dejection is a result of the west wind, which affects the inner ear. After several days of it, energy levels fall, depression sets in, voices drop and, as Synge already noted eighty years ago, 'all is but a murmur'. I'm

acquainted with the *foehn* (the southerly wind that crosses the Swiss Alps) which also has a pernicious effect, making the most cheerful natures irritable, and bringing violence and suicides in its train. Right up to the Restoration, the courts in central Switzerland were not permitted to sit while the *foehn* blew. Since the mid-nineteenth century, thanks to a succession of positivists – scholars or lawyers who disregard nature – this wise provision has been in abeyance.

The barman has also succumbed to this sort of prostrate anaesthesia. He is seated with his arms folded, eyes closed, under a notice that reads: I LOVE MY JOB BUT I HATE THE WORK.

Just as I say to myself, 'What the hell am I doing here?' on a whim of the sky the late-afternoon light suddenly becomes very beautiful, burnishing the mistletoe that still hangs over the door, travelling across some liquids of dubious colours. In short, notwithstanding the poverty of the place, this amber half-light has the effect of those Flemish masters who could reproduce on the side of a carafe the whole tavern that filled their canvases. It is too dark just to snap it. I balance my camera on a little tripod, put it on the corner of the bar and, deceived by the general torpor, don't bother to say the crucial, 'Don't move!' Aperture: 5.6; exposure: one second. That very second they choose to yawn and stretch and blink. Instead of a Vermeer I have a Francis Bacon, with its melted, viscous, liverish shapes. No doubt more faithful to the spirit of the place.

From Kilronan to Eóghanaght, early evening
When I asked the barman how to get to the nearby coast to return to Kilmurvey along the shore, he replied, 'Impossible,' meaning that no one made such a trip on foot and in such weather. Although it was only just two hours away, like good sailors the Aran islanders don't like walking. To move a stone's throw they get on their bikes or hitch up a wagon. An island of carts. I pass a paddock where five foals tied up to a mulberry tree kick and jump to keep themselves warm: you find these donkeys or little mules in backyards almost everywhere, beneath the column of steam rising from their nostrils. They give this port, in its winter sleep, a touch of obstinate liveliness which it really needs.

curlew echoing tin whistle
to eye-swimming melancholy
is that our offering?

John Montague

Walked along for nine kilometres without encountering any signs
of life other than a few coots and small waders, motionless on the
dark waters. Across the bay of Mainistir, where the muddy shore
shines, its green almost black. Overhead the hooded crows – like
those in the Celsus manuscript – dropped mussels and winkles
found among the rocks on to the icy road, breaking their shells.
Crunch of hailstones on the ground, shells fallen from the sky, a
confusion of centuries, medieval miracle! But the birds engaged
in this manoeuvre without the raucous crowing, the rapid diving,
the querulous excitement that usually attend it. The entire bestiary
seemed to be gripped by the same Atlantic neurosis. The wind,
which had the island in its stranglehold behind the brow of the
cliffs, assailed me sometimes head-on, sometimes from behind,
not too strong, cold enough to wipe away my fever, carrying its
powerful odours of seaweed, iodine and rotting reeds.

Black night, the rise and fall of my footsteps on the road
which rings like porcelain, furtive rustling in the rushes (dormice?
Curlews, more likely?); around me there was indeed that promised
'nothing'. Or rather, 'a little', a frugality that reminded me of the
desolate wastelands of north Japan, of the tiny poems, bordering on
silence, written by the seventeenth-century itinerant monk Bashō.
I feel at home in these landscapes made of less, and to walk alone
along a winter road, warm in wool, is a healthy exercise, a kind of
mantra, which gives what is little – inside ourselves or outside – its
chance of being noticed, carefully weighed up, tuned precisely to
the larger score; always present, though our deafness to the world
deprives us of it all too often.

Kilmurvey, the same evening
Found my hosts in a very good mood: the nephew on account of
his morning Venus; the uncle because it was his natural state but
also because he spends half his time in another world, which he

suspects I share in my own way, and he is glad to talk to me about it. They confide what they think of the respective national virtues of their summer guests. They entirely agree as to the laurels. Behind the Americans, who are untouchable for their own reasons, come the Italians.

'Why?' (I love Italy, but a Roman is the last person I can imagine here. Moreover, the Romans never reached Ireland, and this absence, along with the Great Famine of 1846–8, is the most decisive non-event in its history.)

'Because they always enjoy themselves,' the nephew says.

'The English are just a little way behind.'

That brought me up short: surely … surely, Cromwell, the merciless evictions, Sinn Fein, Ulster. They feel far away from these problems. What pleases them is English politeness, and the way they express their satisfaction with everything.

'They are even happy about the rain, they say thank you for a crumb,' says the uncle.

The French? They are difficult to get to know and don't know their own minds. With one exception: 'Last year we had some French people who killed rabbits with sticks or stones and who asked us to cook them… ahem!'

Before the war, they'd eaten rabbits and the meat was much tastier than farmed rabbits, but they hadn't done so for a long time now: a matter of status, an indication of the level of prosperity. Today there are so many rabbits, and it's so easy to shoot them, that people would be ashamed to find one on their plate. They thought the French should keep up with the times.

The Swiss? There are no Swiss in their golden book. I am the first, and they are by no means sure that I am either Swiss or a journalist.

Ate some of the omelette that had just been brought to the table. They were surprised to see me eating. The road had worn me out. When I told them that I'd returned on foot from Kilronan, going as far as the end of the island and back, they didn't believe me. A liar in the land of lies. Yet it was scarcely fifteen kilometres; I hadn't left the bike at the door and you could hear the sound of a motor from over a mile away, thanks to the westerly wind. So? Astride a broomstick? This seemed a much more plausible explanation here. On the other hand, the uncle does believe in my fever and seems to know its nature. In the morning, before I go out – he gets up before me to walk the dogs – and in the evening, when I return, he touches my hands with two fingers and says 'too hot' or 'too cold'. This evening he said 'too hot' and prepared an infusion to bring the temperature to its ideal level. An infusion entirely of his own making, and I asked no questions about it. We'll see: I'm shivering miserably. What matters is that this evening I felt as though I'd met the old man in a previous existence.

Kilmurvey, Sunday afternoon
In Ireland itself I always felt a sense of incompleteness. Something blank, a hole somewhere, like an octave with a missing note, a chessboard where the castles had been taken away. The absence of a sound, a colour, perhaps of a person, gave me the feeling that I'd arrived just a moment too soon, or too late, surprising it in a state of lack. The magnificent popular music of Ireland would be enough to make this uneasiness disappear, but in winter all the good musicians are on the Continent where they can earn a better living.

In Tuscany, in Burgundy, in western Turkey, you come across landscapes which present themselves as complete, as if for inspection, with everything you were waiting for, perhaps even too much. Not here. In the county of Connemara you see the earth turn fleecy in two shades of brown beneath racing clouds and, alone in the middle of a vast horizon, a peasant, as small and black as a cricket, filling a minuscule wagon with black peat. A magnificent painting if Turner were to have passed this way, but a landscape? More of a collection carelessly assembled from the offcuts of landscapes that had seen better days. Even someone who only nibbles at nature – me – will remain hungry. The Irish, poets especially, send you back constantly to this sort of poverty, make you feel it before you can quite put your finger on what it is. In the same way, they excuse their own taste for exaggeration and invention, for which one would not dream of reproaching them, and practise a kind of self-mockery as though to shelter their make-believe from reality (which reality?).

With the exception of the astonishing flowering of religion, philosophy and art from the fifth to the twelfth centuries, a period they have every right to boast about, they readily describe their history as 'in a trough', as a negative: a succession of non-events, entire sections of their patrimony destroyed or removed by invaders, blood-letting that can never be healed or rendezvous that were missed. The Romans *did not occupy* Ireland, thus depriving her of the infrastructure – logical, political, urban, epigraphical – which exists across south-west Europe. Cromwell and his pillagers usually demolished what they couldn't take away. Evictions caused whole villages to disappear. The Great Famine of 1847 emptied the island of three and a half million natives, who died of hunger or went into exile. During the Second World War, with a justifiable resentment that we ignorantly could not account for, the country kept its distance, was suspected by the British Admiralty of providing refuge for German submarines and, four years later, was not to be found in the victors' camp… Four centuries of trials and tribulations have made the Irish so fatalistic that they forget to point out that this frugality, leanness, lack, just as the endless effort to remedy it, can produce something positive and precious.

As you leave the parish of Oughterard, in Galway, in a field beside the road you can see an astonishing semi-circular cavity, a sort of grass bowl close-cropped by sheep, whose edges form a perfect circle and in which you could easily fit a bus. I was there with a teacher given to the kind of black humour I mentioned.

'Do you see that great hole? Once upon a time there was an enormous stone there, as round as a billiard-ball, mentioned in the ancient chronicles, which they took away.'

'Which *they*?'

'The Vikings, the fairies, Cromwell's soldiers… No one has a clue.'

'And what happened to it?'

'Nobody knows.'

Obviously, a granite sphere, especially one this size, is an interesting phenomenon, but not difficult to imagine. You could think of an ice-age pothole, a meteor or even one of the balls from the Byzantine siege engines that you see in false perspective in the Treatises of Apollodorus of Sicily or Leo the Strategist, which are so gigantic that they would never work – the ropes would heat up, the pulleys burst, a humiliated soldier would fall on his sword. Multiply such a ball by a hundred and all curiosity is snuffed out. But this hollowed hemisphere, covered like a billiard table with short, velvety grass which emphasises its sublime roundness, this Memling-green womb, which one would like to crawl to the bottom of and sleep in for ever, is provocative and mysterious in quite another way. People with no conscience and with the upper hand – the Irish often get the worst of it – could certainly steal a large stone and roll it wherever they wanted, but not this marvellous jewel-box that has been left behind.

Sunday night

I wanted to photograph the children in the primary school the next morning, but it was closed during the storm and the teacher had taken the chance to spend a few days in Galway.

'You see the lads on the road with their big satchels,' the uncle said to me, 'the wind will catch sight of them out of the corner of its eye, and whisk them away from us and set them down in Dublin.'

No need of Nils Holgersson's goose.* He still remembers clearly his own schoolbag to which his mother tied a lump of peat, each pupil having to bring their own. Never mind: this evening I have all I need.

Too much fever to sleep, just enough to be pleasantly delirious between the Prussian blue eiderdown, the lamp with its yellow silk tassels, the bare, whitewashed walls. Below me, I hear the nephew dreamily soliloquising, the wind which circles and snores about the house, lingering like a thief by doors and windows. The idea of returning to Europe and my garden beneath a metre of snow was something that no longer displeased me. Add the agreeable bitterness of the infusion. All of this fills my mind to such an extent that, this evening, not even a needle could slip into it.

At a great distance, I see that the hands placed flat on the quilt – mine – are already asleep and the scratches of last night are almost healed. At nineteen, I wanted to make them the hands of a pianist. I didn't have the courage, or life decided otherwise. They have done other things, though: patched up carburettors and camshafts, held an accordion in a bar in Quetta, done the washing-up on the white,

---

* *The Wonderful Adventures of Nils* (1906–7), by Selma Lagerlöf, tells the story of Nils the farmer's son who flies across the whole of Sweden on a goose, learning many lessons as he goes. (Trs.)

defunct liners of shipping companies, handled Pentax and Nikon cameras, chased – of their own volition and in various latitudes – dung flies come to mop my eyes, stroked many a flea-ridden tomcat and some women, lightly traced the curve of an eyebrow with an index finger to keep someone's gaze on me when I really needed to know something. As for music, I will ask for another life which will be given to me so I can devote myself solely to that. Good hands, already a bit speckled, asleep before I am. I fall asleep in a world complete. Carabas.[*]

Monday morning

Within a rifle shot north of this house, at the junction of two sunken lanes, stands a large thatched cottage of grey stone. For sale, already sold? I wouldn't be the buyer. For all its simple, handsome proportions, it is one of the most desolate dwellings I have ever seen. The large rusting tubs which flank the west façade are not water-troughs for sheep. The film-maker Robert J. Flaherty, who bought this building for the duration of his shoot, developed the reels of *Man of Aran* in them as he went along.

At the end of the nineteenth century, at the time of the Irish Revival, Yeats had despatched his young acolyte Synge to Aran to learn Gaelic and to take down the storytellers' repertoire. Synge, who had been living in Paris, went reluctantly. His first stay on the islands was enough to win him over. He returned over the next four years (1898–1902), and waited another five before finding a publisher for his book *The Aran Islands*, which only circulated among Hibernophiles and the initiated. Amongst them was Robert Flaherty, an American film-maker, born in Michigan but of Irish descent. Synge's extremely detailed description of the incredibly laborious and frugal life of the islanders made him curious. Flaherty, whose father had worked in a mine in the Northwoods region of Canada, had spent his childhood in primeval forest and in the company of Indians and Eskimos. After studying geology, at thirty-five he turned towards documentary film, and his first film, *Nanook of the North*, brought him instant fame. He then worked in Polynesia, alone and with Murnau, alone in

---

[*] In Charles Perrault's version of the tale of *Puss in Boots*, the Marquis de Carabas is the cat's master, whose title and fortune owe everything to the cat's ingenuity. (Trs.)

England, and disembarked on Aran for reconnaissance at the end of 1931, accompanied by his wife and three lovely daughters. He was then forty-eight, a blue-eyed giant, his hair already white. It was the beginning of an adventure which would last two years and which all the old people on the island remember to this day. And the start of a misunderstanding.

Michael has invited me to see the film, of which he has a cassette, at the house of his parents: two old people, translucent and delicate as milk-glass, sitting by the fireside in a room of Presbyterian austerity. He has a job registering bags at the airport (if it must really be called that); she knits those matchless pullovers for which the summer visitors queue. *Man of Aran*, which I hadn't seen for forty years, had lost none of its magic. Flaherty had found the islands almost the same as when Synge had left them thirty years before. Their self-sufficiency was even harsher because, after the Depression, America had cut back on immigration and thus the New York lung was no longer working. He had spent two years refining his material to make barely an hour of film, which covers the four seasons of Inishmore, shows the incredibly violent Atlantic weather that I'd experienced since my arrival, and the poverty and harshness of daily life before it entirely disappeared. In the old days, the light curraghs which rise and fall like corks in the most gigantic swell, and require prodigious skill to hold face-on to the waves, were put out to sea in winter as in summer, which is no longer the case. In the old days, they blessed the winter storms which uprooted seaweed from the depths and deposited it by the ton on the shore. One of the main island resources, it was used not only for smoking and for building up fields, but once dried, was also sold as manure along the coast of Galway; above all, in June each family built ovens on the beach where the seaweed was burnt to provide blocks of soda, which were then broken up and exported to the mainland to be made into soap. The process was quite a business: the ovens had to be watched day and night, the oxygen supply reduced or increased to achieve sufficient combustion. Each family had its own recipe and knack. Replaced today by more reliable and less expensive industrial production, this activity, too, has disappeared. Flaherty presented the 'works and days' of the islanders very well… and added some elements which were foreign to them. He was a storyteller who started out with one reality and then embroidered it as he pleased; the Irish should be the last to reproach him for such bias. Thus he included in the film a scene of hunting a basking shark, which the islanders hadn't done for sixty years, as it was not profitable enough and above all too costly in human lives. He sent emissaries to Donegal, where they still hunted these monsters, to find out about the length of the harpoons, the iron barbs and the spot where they struck their prey. The islanders got involved and, at great danger to themselves, slaughtered the shark, which was no longer accustomed to feeling afraid in their waters.

Flaherty had huge difficulties in assembling his main actors and extras. In these islands where they believed – and still believe – in innumerable forms of occult interference, the camera could be an evil eye. Moreover, it was feared that women and children could lose their religion working for a man who did not say his prayers and in connection with whom 'socialism' was mentioned under the breath. By means of tact, stubbornness and genuine interest in the islanders' life, he succeeded in convincing them that his endeavour had nothing satanic about it; the refinement and intelligence of his wife, who was very popular on Inishmore, did the rest.

When he finally got his cast in place – the father, the mother, the son and the curragh crews – Flaherty, in his ignorance of the sea, made them run risks that would be incredible today, and that his 'actors' out of defiance and bravado accepted, grumbling. The worse the weather, the more he wanted to film it. In a terrifying storm sequence you see the mother, her hair dishevelled, jump into enormous waves to save her husband, whose boat has overturned on him, and she – a superb, wild actress – is within a hair's breadth of drowning. It is impossible to watch these scenes today without thinking that they were rigged: they were not; that shipwreck was not anticipated.

'I remember it well,' says the father. 'I was there, I had a little part as an extra, halfway up the cliff. We all tumbled down towards the beach, seeing what was happening. That wasn't expected either. It's a miracle that film was completed without loss of life. That woman, Maggie – the mother – is still alive. She only leaves her bed for two hours each morning and doesn't want to see anybody any more. She thinks the whole world has seen her in that minute of agony and that she's been cheated. Anyway, she doesn't want to hear any more talk about it.'

The film was shown in London, at the New Gallery, in April 1934. The main characters were there, invited over from Aran by Flaherty. When the public recognised them, sitting in a box, they gave them a standing ovation. They were all seeing London for the first time. The Flahertys gave them a royal tour: the Tower of London, Madame Tussauds, and finally a circus from which they emerged convinced that if the horses were real horses, then the equestrians were some of the *sidhe* (fairy creatures) because they were more often aloft than in the saddle or with their feet on the ground. Pat Mullen, an islander who was Flaherty's assistant and factotum for the whole of the shoot, recounts in his memoirs that nothing would dissuade them. All the same many of them, reading the rave reviews that Flaherty sent over, were convinced that he had made a fabulous profit at their expense. They took the boat to the cinema in Galway to see Tarzan and Robin Hood swing from branch to branch, hanging from creepers, and considered those gymnastics a picnic compared to the risks they'd taken among the breakers of a raging sea and that they at least deserved the rate earned by a 'stuntman'.

They were mistaken: Flaherty had devoted two years of his life to making them known, doing real justice to the rough nobility he found here. He had put almost all the money his previous films had made him into the enterprise. He was paying them adequately, if you take into account the context, the period and the modest way he lived himself. Those who had known how to look after this manna had been able to buy the houses and plots of land that they had only held as tenants. The others, spendthrifts, resented him. Flaherty, far from making a fortune, had to go to an oil company to finance his last film, *Louisiana Story*, and despite its success he did not become rich. Meanwhile Ireland had come through the Second World War, in what was seen as suspicious neutrality, and some of those who had seen the film came to see the islands out of curiosity. It was not yet tourism, but it was a beginning. When Flaherty returned to Aran at the end of the 1940s, he received a lukewarm welcome. Some of his friends came to meet him at the jetty, others shut the door in his face. He must have been hurt by this misunderstanding and did not extend his stay. After *Louisiana Story*, his masterpiece, he gave up the cinema and died three years later, in 1951…

… The cassette finished with the sight of three men abandoning a curragh, panic-stricken, and scrambling sideways like crabs on the rocks, before a huge wave reduces their craft to matchwood. And this is not *cinema*. We all had tears in our eyes. The father threw another peat on the fire and said: 'I think he was completely honest, just worked in a different way from us. Anyway, he put these islands on the map of Europe; before him, no one knew we existed.'

I had thought that we'd spend the afternoon sipping poteen – an illegal white whiskey made by the people of Connemara and which they drink quite openly here – but I was wide of the mark. My friend and his parents belong to a Church of Scotland sect which does not allow drinking or smoking. During the Great Famine, the Scots, themselves exiles in Ulster after the Clearances, who had recovered through hard work, rigour and frugality, had come to the areas of the West of Ireland that were most affected, and opened canteens to feed their Catholic compatriots in the hope – dashed, of course – of converting the most starved of the recipients. Many of them had remained in the west and put down roots. Some had crossed over to the islands where they had been made very welcome. It was an Anglican priest, indeed, who did the first serious work on the Aran 'forts' and dated them accurately, as it turned out. Whether one is Catholic, Baptist or Presbyterian, alcohol is strongly disapproved of here: it's a whim for which nature exacts too dear a payment. As with us in the high mountains, it's too dangerous. To walk along a vertiginous goat-track in the winter, or to keep a curragh facing the waves in a high sea is not an exercise you can survive for long if your nose is always in a glass, and if you take a wave on the beam and it fills the boat, you are more than likely to end up in the cemetery, in the little corner for drunks. Thus, they don't drink unless the wind along the coast prevents the boats going out. You don't see drunkards here, although they're the only ones who would venture out in such a mad wind. In fact, since my arrival on the island, I haven't spoken to more than eight people, which suits me fine.

Left Michael's house at nightfall and walked as far as the cemetery by the bay of Kileany. A magnificent view of the restless, black-satin sea. Wandered between the graves, which I lit up with my pocket torch: purple-beaded wreaths, which I like and which can be found –

like pairs of magpies – from here to the Urals; hideous china cherubs, fattened, ageless cupids with cunning expressions. Pity to be done up in such bad taste, when the body is undone and has departed elsewhere! There were indeed a few graves grouped together on a separate plot. I read the inscriptions: all were sailors who died at sea, but there was no indication that alcohol had been involved. I believe that Michael had invented this story out of his own inclination towards austerity and mortification. Returned by night along the melancholy north road. On my left, more than three miles away, I could hear the drumming of the sea against the cliffs. At the house, all were sleeping. Up in my room I looked at the map. Today I had walked nearly twenty kilometres without noticing, in a sort of intoxication. The tiredness would perhaps get the better of the fever: we must tire out the illnesses that visit us; usually they will let go before the body does.

Kilmurvey, Tuesday morning

> All the perversions of the soul
> I learnt on a small farm.
> How to do the neighbours harm
> by magic, how to hate.
>
> Michael Hartnett

 I heard the nephew and the uncle pass each other the telephone, or rather, wrench it from one another. It was easy to work out that it was the friend from Dublin who had found me this room, and was calling for my news. They had to tell her that I was still asleep. So I made it look as though I was, cast as 'the stranger on the island in winter'.

The nephew: 'He doesn't eat any of my cooking, at night he paces round his room, he spends the days on the road or at the foot of the cliffs.'

The uncle: 'He's feverish by night and lively by day. His hands are burning or freezing. This isn't a journalist, he's written hardly anything.' (That's true.) And he finished, laughing, 'He's one of the *sidhe*.'

He had already told me how he had lost an elder brother who was bewitched and for him, the existence of the Other World was self-evident.

The reader will say, 'Here come the fairies! It's true that in Ireland there's no getting away from them.'

It's not about fairies, but here – exactly because the Romans never came – the supernatural and strange are an integral part of everyday troubles. I don't say this out of an infatuation with the occult. 'You aren't moved to become a magus by some romantic notion: you either are one or you aren't. Most often, you're not,' as Charles-Albert Cingria wrote with his usual insight. I am not one, but here – as in Korea and Tibet – they exist, a bit more often than elsewhere. Life is a game of snakes and ladders where one incessantly moves from the reasonable to the imaginary – which is powerful, nourished, taken into account. We must not be misled by the extreme complexity of Celtic mythology or by the inconstancy of its heroes – who get out of bed on the right side and redress wrongs by day, and at night turn into parricides or adulterers – which unsettles our Manicheanism and sometimes leaves the reader behind. First of all, these reversals and denials are part of our nature, and then it doesn't need a crystal ball to work out that much of this complexity and duplication has been tacked on, since these legends have been recorded, lost and rewritten a hundred times, so that sense has been lost and parts have been added and embroidered, diluting the effect and the venom. In Ireland's golden age, the ink was hardly dry on the page of a monk-copyist before a Viking would emerge from his longboat, or a visitor from the other world, intent on destroying it or taking it away. The *Lebor Gabála Érenn* – 'The Book of Invasions' – a twelfth-century recension of an undoubtedly much older chronicle recounting the invasions of historical figures and others… mentions, besides the four provinces of Ulster, Connaught, Leinster and Munster, a fifth county which is the underworld, the *sidhe*. Access to this world is through the graves (*shid*) of the island's first occupants, who had been conquered by the Celts at the beginning of the first century BC and who hid underground – in grottos, tombs, springs – whence they emerged when they saw fit to take their revenge or demand justice, taking the shape – human, animal, vegetable – that best suited their plans. The medieval Irish texts try – though not very convincingly – to define and especially to limit the powers of these vanquished ghosts.

On Aran, where everything is passed on through the oral tradition, the intrigues and misdemeanours of these underground neighbours are reported in a language that is more direct, current and moreover more menacing because the tellers were often on the receiving end. What makes the tales one can hear on the island powerful is their simplicity. It is a mistake to think that when life doesn't consist of much, people embroider. On the contrary, with a wind of fourteen on the Beaufort Scale which condemns the islanders to silence three months out of twelve, there's no time for embroidering, they go straight to essentials. There is a parallel world. There are creatures who emerge from it, sometimes they love you, sometimes they help you, but more often they carry you off or kill you. Under-age boys are the most at risk. On the island of Inishmaan, just south of Inishmore, Synge witnessed this: one day in winter 1901, a strange woman dressed in city clothes comes up the village street, sees a boy playing in front of a cottage, looks at him and says softly, 'What a beautiful little boy.' The mother, immediately on her guard, wants to spit on the child's head to ward off a spell but her mouth is dry. She wants to say, 'God bless him,' but she has a lump in her throat. The same evening, the child has a wound on his neck, is delirious, and says that he's leaving for America. In the store cupboard, the seed-potatoes are covered in blood. The same night, the bewitched child dies. The unknown woman has of course disappeared in smoke. Seen, chosen, bewitched, killed: as simple as a telegram.

Here they call these visitors the *good people*, ironically, in order to appease their anger. Right up to the Second World War they dressed boys as girls to fool these good people. The uncle told me that until he was four or five he wasn't allowed to cross the threshold alone, and that he was always tripping over his pinafore. Pat Mullen, Flaherty's assistant, wore a tweed skirt with the hem let down a bit more each year until he reached puberty. Through lazy habit these good people, most often female, were referred to as 'fairies', which suggests cardboard cut-outs of maidens in headdresses, armed with wands which emit a shower of sparks. False. The good people can take the shape of whatever will deceive. Here, the most common visitors are small girls about one and a half feet high, who rise from the ground at nightfall and dance in a circle in hollows in the dunes. According to the uncle, who has seen them twice, they wear a kind of Phrygian cap which covers their eyebrows. They're said to own about a tenth of the island's wealth and to be as mean as snakes, but occasionally they fall in love with a man and make his fortune. It is they who, in various disguises, steal boys, killing them or bringing them up underground to be their lovers, because their erotic hunger is in no way constrained by their small stature. The captives grow old and grey in satisfying the appetites and whims of these childish mistresses, who themselves do not age. Sometimes they send their companions back into the world again, to obtain some information, deliver a message, return a gift or perform some dirty trick. These emissaries look no different from you or me. The thing that might mark them out to the watchful eye is an old-fashioned item of elegance in their clothing – a yellow satin waistcoat, silver buckles on their shoes – but above all they are given away by their stammer when they have to say – which happens all the time here – the name of a mutual friend, cousin, some relation. When they are touched by daylight, these imposters disappear like a puff of steam.

They wouldn't get past the uncle's vigilance for long. He added, 'You just have to keep your eyes peeled,' staring at me knowingly (by the way, why say that to me?), and declared that he wasn't at all afraid of the *sidhe*. He talked about them much as a *Baedeker* would describe the Boboli Gardens. Moreover, the auspicious places he knew about were effective against bad luck, as long as you got to them in time. Before his departure for America, at the beginning of the 1930s, someone who felt him or herself to be a victim of some occult plot would seek out a woman from Kileany who would say, 'Go to such and such a place, look under such and such a stone and bring me back a white pebble and a black root,' or heaven knows what; afterwards, you had to kill a cock or a sheep and the evil spell would be reduced to water.

The presence and constant incursions of the good people were a worry and a headache for the parish priests of Ireland over the centuries. Since they couldn't be got rid of, they had to be fitted into the Holy Scriptures somewhere. The solution they found reeks of patches and panic. I only give it here in order to get shot of it: when Lucifer and his mutinous band tumbled from heaven like balls of lead, an archangel intercepted them so that those who were still in the air would be suspended rather than fall into the infernal cauldrons. They floated there, almost within earshot, unsure of their fate and, according to Synge, causing havoc. The Celtic version is far more illuminating: this defeat, this unjust division, this fools' bargain is contested by 'the others', who torment the Irish without respite and sow bad feeling amongst them. Impossible to open a paper – even the racing papers – without finding some trace of these troublemakers.

For the nephew, this legend was already rubbish. Not for everyone. When these shades finally lose their empire, they will retain the ultimate power of the ghosts of Japanese folklore: pick any story and, grumbling, tell just a little bit of it to send a child who's bawling or contrary off to bed dumb with fright.

Kilronan, Tuesday afternoon
A break in the storm. Tonight there's a flight for Galway. I've packed my bag, said goodbye to my hosts, and set out for Kilronan. The grocer's is open for the first time. I love grocer's shops, they provide a moral inventory of a place. A deep silvery bell, as loud as the station bells of yesteryear, marked my entry but summoned no one. I looked around; besides the tins of tea, tuna and sardines which you expect in this sort of place, there were: plaits of chewing tobacco; horrible portraits of John Paul II on varnished red wood; a large china bowl full of wrinkled apples (five pence each); green eggs flecked with black from I know not what seabird; cylindrical whetstones, more practical than ours, which are quadrangular; an enormous demijohn of white whiskey, upside down and provided with a valve so that it could be served by the measure to customers; long socks of oiled wool in shades of indigo, and those lighters with a tinder wick which only really work in a strong wind…

I was at that point of my inspection when I heard the cheerful sound of a flush being pulled. The grocer appeared: brisk, freckled, her hair tightly curled, her blue-green eyes darting. She had a little cross of soot on her forehead, and said by way of a friendly greeting: 'Ashes to ashes and dust to dust.' I remarked that she was a day ahead of Ash Wednesday, and that she should wait until tomorrow. She laughed, spat into her palm, and wiped it off. I thus understood I was the first customer of the day. Over the counter there was one of those notices I'd come to like:

WE KNOW THAT EVERYBODY HAS A PROBLEM
BUT WE DON'T WANT TO HEAR ABOUT IT.

I wanted to buy the sign but she wouldn't sell it to me, assuring me – an Irish fib – that I'd find the same one in Galway. That wasn't really a problem. But after those fevered days she had left me with a puzzle, presented by her untimely mistake: *Ashes to ashes and dust to dust.* There was something wrong in that funereal saying: with such a wind, nothing returns to nothing. One more lie? Most probably.

Scotland: Travels in the Lowlands

Foreign freebooter, inept and ill [...]
Who are you, blown here by Scythian winds?
So many have come this way by land or by sea.

Guillaume Apollinaire

Published in 1988, Écosse – pierre, vent et lumière (Scotland – stone, wind and light) *is a collection of essays selected by the Scottish writer and poet of 'geopoetics' Kenneth White, a long-time resident of France. He wanted to revive the 'Auld Alliance', the Franco-Scottish exchange which dates back centuries, by including both Scottish and French writers, and placed Bouvier's essay at the beginning of the book, no doubt because it evokes those elements of stone and light so powerfully. It is the work of a very alert and open traveller, who had been reading Scottish authors – Walter Scott, Robert Louis Stevenson – since his childhood, and who could see past the 'half-truths and caricatures' that White wanted to displace, to the complexities and distinctiveness of Scottish culture. And as Bouvier wrote in* The Way of the World, *the traveller has to be prepared to be 'undone' by his journeying – if not, why bother to travel?*

Many years ago, in India, I came across an article in a glossy magazine headed 'Practical advice for those wanting to go to Ceylon'. The advice consisted of one sentence: 'Give up this stupid plan immediately and go salmon fishing in Scotland instead.' The rest of the article was about the Highlands.

It came back to me, somewhat belatedly. Meanwhile I spent a year in Ceylon, where I barely held on to what remained of my reason. I've never been salmon fishing, and aged almost sixty, I'm discovering Scotland this evening, looking out of my window on to the dark street, in the heart of this capital new to me, where I know no one, where I arrived without preparation or a plan but with sciatica brought back from my last trip to China, which causes me to stop every hundred metres, grimacing.

The Scots must have had a whistling bird as a totemic ancestor. The lifts here, for example, don't ring as they arrive, they whistle familiarly right in your ear. The police cars and ambulances don't hoot as in New York or screech as in Paris, they whistle like blackbirds. On the pavement beneath my window, youths in white T-shirts emerge befuddled from the pub, whistle to hail a taxi, and whistle again, twice as loud, when the driver, judging that they will throw up on the seats, reverses and quickly slips away. This latter whistle, supposed to make the driver feel ashamed, is accompanied by the V-sign and shouting. After several fruitless attempts, the group splits up and each makes his unsteady way in the direction his clouded mind suggests. Just then, the whistling of the kettle makes me jump. All hotel rooms here, even the simplest, provide the means for making tea.

Random items seen at the Antiques Fayre on George Street: a pair of cracked boots in poor repair, with a ducal monogram. White china ashtrays from the 1920s, quite impractical, in the shape of Vauban's forts. Also a sponge-ware rat dressed like a Dickensian lawyer, with a fob watch hanging from his waistcoat. The enamelled buttons of various railway companies, now defunct. Boxes for stiff collars, made of polished leather in British India, where the Scots were always put in the frontline to be peppered by Pathans (see Kipling). Fine turn-of-the-century silverware, plain and sturdy with good hallmarks, from the little port of Oban. Plates by Aubrey Beardsley taken from an Oscar Wilde first edition. Seascapes, seascapes – in gouache, charcoal, watercolour – as if the whole country were nothing but coastline, mist, light showers, sudden rainbows…

… But above all: an atmosphere of jollity and cheerfulness that makes the Scots excellent shopkeepers. Moreover, the prices are very reasonable. I spot a pretty Victorian pillbox in agate with gilding. I want to buy it for a lady who adores such things.

'How much?'

'Ten pounds.'

'Is it of any use to bargain, or is it hopeless?'

The ageless, red-haired woman behind the little stall seems to be very comfortable with her place in the world. She laughs (the French accent makes the Scots laugh, but they don't forget that they were faithful allies of the French monarchy for five centuries) and looks in her notebook for the price she paid.

'I'm afraid you'll still have to pay eight.'

In another shop on George Street, I buy one of those shooting-sticks that opens to make a stool so that I can sit down anywhere when the sciatica strikes. I have to learn to travel with this stick and this constant threat. My sudden sit-downs amuse the Edinburgh dustmen, who think that I've stopped for a chat and immediately begin speaking in a patois I can barely understand.

The sky suddenly clouds over, but the city loses none of its festive air. There are kilted bagpipers busking almost everywhere; old ladies in straw hats, out enjoying themselves, are photographed with them, arms around their waists. On a perfect lawn in Princes Gardens, below Princes Street which is only built up on one side, golfers have fun putting, paying no heed to the rain as it begins to fall. The carefree atmosphere and elegant Georgian architecture of the New Town is like a counterweight to the sombre, winding mass of the Old Town rising opposite, dominated by its black fortress which suggests murder and intrigue. A double city, whose ambiguous nature is expressed in Stevenson's *Dr Jekyll and Mr Hyde*.

At Edinburgh Castle you can see an enormous cannon known affectionately as Mons Meg (it was cast in Mons), undoubtedly the largest in fifteenth-century Europe. It has been reassembled after having exploded several times. If we're to believe the audio-visual guide which recounts its history, full of din and smoke, this monster hasn't often rendered the services expected of it. Only once has its hefty cannonball struck home and, amid cheers, demolished the walls of a treacherous lord. Twice it has preferred to backfire, turning the powdermen and even a Scottish king into a shower of bloody fragments. The beginnings of artillery are yet another example of our unfathomable stupidity. Tactically, the huge pieces of ordnance served no purpose. These toys were often lethal to the powerful men who prided themselves on owning them. While Mons Meg was sowing terror or disappointment in its own camp, at the other end of the world the Mughal Emperor Babur was making the same offensive experiments with the cannons he'd had made to raze the Rajput citadels: with a thunderclap, the cannonball got as far as the mouth of the cannon and fell literally at the feet of the head powdermen. Babur – who was a very good man – had to heap them with compliments to stop them from falling on their swords.

On the walls of the blockhouse – Mons Meg occupies almost the whole of its length – excellent sketches (Scottish curators are generous with sketches) show that it was as dangerous to make as to use a cannon. You see about thirty yokels busy with long pliers or ladles around the forges and crucibles, faces covered with rags against the poisonous vapours. You guess that some of the kids who are to be seen in their shirtsleeves gnawing on crusts, even on the clay floor of the foundry, are soon going to fall into the furnace or maim themselves with red-hot pliers. From Mons Meg to Big Bertha, these gigantic cannon have only served to bring misery to the poor. The great bells which were rung, for example, when the cannon ceased and were just as difficult to cast, served a different end. Especially the heaviest and deepest sounding, which – since Newton's revelations – no longer make the journey to Rome to be blessed at Easter, and remain fast in their bell-tower, for the pleasure of the descendants of Luther, Calvin and John Knox.

Leaving Mons Meg, you open your umbrella to climb a slippery, cobbled ramp, cross a courtyard and enter a little military museum, which demonstrates beyond any argument that the Scots have always had a taste for brawling, and for the striking and muted colours (the more violent the action, the more hushed the colour) proper to northern cultures – those which make the costume of the Lapps, for instance, so beautiful. Here you find all the uniforms, surcoats, doublets, redingotes, breeches, thigh-boots, jodhpurs, kilts, helmets, shakos, berets, caps, braiding, sabretaches that the Scots have worn since they took up arms (which wasn't yesterday). You will also notice that several services or regiments wore the 'Wellington red and gold' which caught no one unawares, and which was simply a concession to the very unequal union of the Crowns.

Where they were able to choose their own colours, however, quite a different aesthetic register is revealed: more magical, less worldly. There is an Ayrshire regimental uniform from around 1840: black tunic and trousers braided in deep green, with dull gold frogging, black and green forage cap, turned up at the back with an aigrette of grouse feathers. You feel that this extraordinarily elegant and funereal costume is not made for 'triumphal entries' but rather (as the Pathan proverb goes) 'to live, to roam, to die, to be forgotten'. It is an outfit for adventure, travel and mourning. The little yellowed photographs attest that this regiment had blown its bagpipes in places as distant from Kilmarnock as the Transvaal, Auckland and Quetta. These colours, taken from the moors and paraded across the world, express the double nature of this country: passionately regionalist and cosmopolitan in its destiny.

Those who wore this uniform did not always do so by choice. Crofters evicted by their sheep-raising landlords or labourers who were victims of the early cotton crises often had no other recourse but to put themselves in an antipodean firing-line for the sake of *Rule, Britannia!*: with homesickness almost equal to that of the Swiss mercenaries of yesteryear, whose graves are to be found, scattered according to conflicts and alliances, from the Moluccas to Ontario; with nostalgia that wipes out all sense of proportion. In Berwick, just on the border with England, they say that an old man, gone grey in harness in the Indian Army and returned to his country, looked

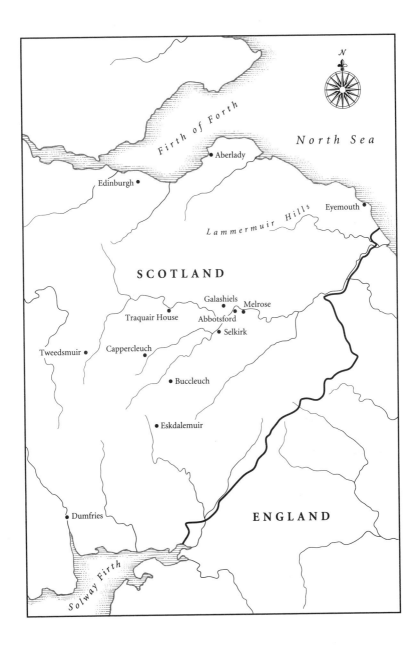

at the banks of the Tweed, murmuring: 'To think that I told them over there that it was wider than the Ganges! What a damned liar I was.' This combination of rootedness and exile reminds me a great deal of my small country, anchored in its customs and mountains... and also one of the most nomadic in the world.

I left the Castle at nightfall, and went back down the Lawnmarket. In less than five hundred metres you find restaurants offering all the world's cuisines. It was raining hard. On the pavements, beneath umbrellas, there were people of every hue who had come perhaps from Stevenson's Samoa, or Mungo Park's Zambezi, cursing the climate in their incomprehensible dialects. And I felt at home.

This morning I left the city like a bed in which I hadn't really slept. I will return when I'm more of a city-dweller. There's an art to living there, I feel – the continental Romantics praised Edinburgh – that I'll be able to understand better once I've seen what nurtured it: a lot of empty space and changing light; a lot of time that goes by without being asked to account for it, unless it offers one a daydream from which death is never absent and which is never forced to translate itself into words – music seems better able to convey it. All this fancy is made solid in the urban fabric, just as the fog is transformed (when necessary) into hail, just as a spoonful of dreaming mixed with one of homely realism turns into mayonnaise.

A weird town: the black fortress built on the site of an ancient, barbarian *dun*, destroyed and rebuilt several times, whose weighty stones sweat, and whose vennels and little winding lanes seep from it like sweat or blood; and right opposite, the 'New' Town, built according to a rational plan during the best period of British urban architecture (the early nineteenth century), grand, light, elegant, erudite – especially the famous anatomy school (medical students dug up the dead and snatched bodies from the gallows before they were cold). It's like a challenge taken up, thumbing the nose at overwhelming England, whose only merit was having been organised (straight roads, bridges, civil engineering, prefects, sub-prefects, the architecture expressing this hierarchy) by Rome.

Reasonably judging that it had neither the capacity nor any interest in managing or administering these mists and moors, Rome did not venture north of what their historians called Northumbria. Following just about the line we call the Border today, they built a series of ditches and small forts mysteriously called 'Cat's tail' or 'Cat's trail'.*

Scotland thus had to wait for its towns until the establishment of Christian foundations, firstly by monks from Ireland – the Irish brain-drain in this period is alarming: all their theological Einsteins were exported – and then by the Benedictines who came over in the tenth–eleventh century from Picardy, invited by the Scottish kings (the beginning of the Auld Alliance), and who constructed a superb necklace of abbeys in south-west Scotland. Henry VIII and John Knox, for different reasons, went about destroying and changing these in the sixteenth century, leaving mere ruins and skeletons, which today sit among perfect lawns and dignified, towering trees which were no bigger than acorns when these buildings suffered wrack and ruin.

The Scotland of towns and markets developed around these abbeys, because the monks knew how to do everything – brew beer, calculate the span of a keystone or of a note of Gregorian chant, plait a sail rope; because they were the only ones who knew how to read; and God, in a way, repaid them for their encyclopaedic labours. How else were they to sell this strange story of a God Father who sacrifices his God Son on a cross to free us from the sins which he had deliberately allowed us to commit? A story with, to my knowledge, no equivalent in Celtic mythology? They needed to pair this story with some good recipes for tisanes to sooth swollen stomachs, or for pitch to seal rowing-boats. These worldly things gave rise to the markets which developed precisely because there were monks on hand who knew how to calibrate Roman scales to weigh leeks or parsley. The only knowledge from the Rome

---

* In fact the Romans built the Antonine Wall considerably farther north, stretching from Old Kilpatrick on the west coast of Scotland to near Bo'ness in the east and about thirty-seven miles long. The remains of a Roman bath-house can still be seen in Bearsden, about four miles north of Glasgow's West End. It also seems that NB was mistaken in ascribing the 'Catrail' to the Romans: although the period of this earthwork is not assigned, the *Object Name Book of the Ordnance Survey* (1861) describes the 'Catrail or Picts' Work Ditch' as the 'remains of a trenched fortification which runs through the Counties of Roxburgh and Selkirk. … In some districts the fortification is known as the Picts work ditch, but in this County it is well known as the Catrail, a name which is said in British to signify the Dividing Fence.' (Trs.)

Christianised by Constantine which does not seem to have been passed on, or perhaps did not interest these great architects of vaults, was the art of bridge-building. We know that the scholar-monks of Melrose Abbey crossed the River Tweed at a ford, on tall stilts, in order to reach their medicinal gardens and pear orchards.

Followed the coast as far as Aberlady. The grey, restless sea must be only thirteen degrees, and is bordered with small 'seaside' towns of neat Victorian cottages, well-to-do but all encrusted with soot and sea-salt and overcome by the immense boredom of Sunday. No one out walking, some motionless figures at the windows. A melancholy atmosphere, as though frozen, like something by Valéry Larbaud. I expect to see him with his pencil lifted, his nose pressed to a window, writing, 'After I have been dead for several years [...] the cabs bumping into each other in the fog.' No cabs here, but a drenched hitchhiker whom I took on board and who explained the landscape to me: the rolling, soaked meadows lifted here and there by gentle hills, crowned with pines and black rocks which come from ancient volcanoes. He was a forestry student going back to the Cheviots where they are reforesting huge areas of grazing land, to the rage of the sheep farmers and for the benefit of the landowners, who claim a subsidy of three pounds per tree planted.

In a lay-by I handed my passenger on to a van going south and, feeling hungry, began to look out for an inn. The first one I found presented an odd sight: behind closed glass doors, the waiters were lovingly arranging white, glossy cylinders, which I at first took for anti-tank shells, on long tables. They were monstrous leeks, washed, pearl-bright, carefully denuded of their rootlets, and placed on the table in bunches with a flag giving each grower's name. The waiters signalled that they wouldn't be open until 12.30, after the jury had arrived, and indeed beribboned medals were waiting on a little table. In the villages of central Japan I had happened on scarecrow competitions (the most horrible won a demijohn of saké, which soon induced collective drunkenness) and once, even, a competition for making faces. It was the first time I'd seen one for leeks. Once I knew about them, I saw they were all the rage this season: the winner was escorted home with car-horns blaring, like a bride. Not having any garden produce in the car, I would therefore have been served last, supping on leftovers with a long spoon.

I returned to the car and went off to find lunch in Eyemouth, because the name intrigued me and because I like ports. This one is built on the west bank of a deep, narrow channel. Steep hills covered in coarse grass rose almost vertically from the east bank. Tunny-boats, trawlers, herring-boats and smaller vessels, moored side by side, covered the entire surface of the water, in a magnificent mix of colours, looking as though they'd been set down in a meadow. At the end of the canal, from a small shipyard, came the brisk song of hammers on a fine hull of light wood, even though it was Sunday. A patch of blue sky was beginning to widen, criss-crossed by the deafening screech of seagulls and other large seabirds dotted about on the yardarms and coiled ropes. The town (two or three thousand inhabitants I'd say) stretches between the open sea and the canal, with its houses of handsome, slate-grey stone and little gardens full of chrysanthemums and dahlias. The whole place was so invigorating and pleasant that if I hadn't been commissioned to investigate the Borders, I would have settled down there for a week or so and invented my travels, or copied out extracts from some romantic travellers whose books were no doubt drowsing in the local library, in the sturdy red and gold bindings of John Murray. As it was, I'd have to dream about it while eating.

I was not the only one to have such a good opinion of Eyemouth, however: the two pubs on the seafront were packed with families from all along the north-east coast in their Sunday best, together with a crowd of rowdy kids in scarves (it was cool), whose cries were luckily drowned out by those of the seagulls. I shifted to make room for a couple in their fifties and went on making notes as I watched. She, a faded platinum blonde, with beautiful green eyes and the slightly vulgar liveliness and sociability of someone who has run a bar or a brothel. He, bald and square-set, with high cheekbones in a lobster-pink face, spoke an English as foursquare as himself; each syllable bounced off his tongue like a wagon on a road full of potholes. Unlike most couples their age, they still had a great deal to say to each other, and at intervals slapped each other heartily on the back.

From behind their beers they regarded me with affable curiosity, as though I had a bone through my nose. I liked the look of them and was wondering how to introduce myself – which I find difficult – when the man addressed me.

'You Jewish?'

'No, why?'

'You're writing in Hebrew!'

'No, I'm writing in French.' (I'm left-handed and my writing looks Gothic or Carolingian, so I understood his mistake.)

'He's Jewish,' said the woman, elbowing him in the ribs affectionately and winking at me, 'a Polish Jew.' And a cod-fisherman in Gdansk since he was sixteen. In 1958 he got to a Danish port and made a break for it, reached Scotland, and moved from cod to herring. He'd been in Eyemouth three years now, married for two, and for six months he'd been fishing on a herring-boat – the latest model, it could go out in any weather. The catches were good and so was the pay. He was on paid leave for a few days because they'd finished running-in the machines and had to tighten some gaskets and grease some valves.

'And she's a Scottish tart,' he said amiably, digging her in the ribs.

She laughed. She didn't work any longer, she'd made her nest-egg and settled down. When he wasn't at sea, they went trout-fishing together on the banks of the Yarrow, a hundred miles south. She concocted little dishes for him and had been badly burnt by the new oven he'd just given her. She had an oozing dressing on her right elbow.

I ordered three beers to drink to this long-awaited honeymoon that promised to last. I looked at him: fisherman, Jew and Scot (naturalised twenty years ago), three characteristics I'd never linked in my mind and now found united in the man facing me, lifting his glass. Fisherman and Jew because we have pigeonholed the Jews so strictly as intellectuals or bankers that it is hard to imagine them with a plough or a net in their hands. Still, four of the apostles were fishermen, and Christ knew enough about fish to make them multiply. Jew and Scot because, from the Continent, Scotland seems too far away, too withdrawn, distinctive, provincial to have its Disraelis, its Rothschilds, its Einsteins as in London or Germany. Yet Ivanhoe saved the beautiful Sarah from the witches' stake. Mendelssohn is an honorary citizen of Fingal's Cave, and of course Shylock... maybe? Perhaps also because the stories that mock both nations give them an equal reputation for meanness, and thus the phrase 'Scottish Jew' seems tautologous, so we unconsciously reject it. Yet neither nation is greedy; what they have in common is knowing how to count, which is quite a different thing. To count as you give is more praiseworthy than 'to give without counting', because then you are conscious of how much you are depriving yourself of and, above all, you can then give regularly (as the Talmud and Maimonides recommend). I was not allowed to pay for the round I'd ordered. For the first time in my fifty-eight years of life, I had met a Scottish Jew and couldn't even manage to buy him a drink. Who was mocking whom?

'Do you want to be the "Herring Queen"?'
'Oh yuck!'
'All right, you're the "Apple Queen".'
They elect a Herring Queen each year here, chosen from among the thirty or so girls who are finishing Eyemouth High School. It is the Queen who christens the boats with champagne as they leave the boatyard, and gives a speech welcoming them to the sea. She also opens the ball when the town holds its festival.

I'm in the little museum beside the church, melancholy and marvellous. Marvellous because *small is beautiful* and because the smaller the museum, the more eloquent the articles on display. And melancholy because at least half the objects you can see here were found on sailors washed up by the sea or commemorate in naïve embroidery or children's drawings the storm of 1881, which left a hundred and eighty-nine dead from this small community. The Herring Queens all have their portraits made, and there is a gallery of photographs starting in the late 1940s, many of which have already turned yellow. In 1952 it was Myriam Maltmann who is seen swinging a bottle at the bow of a fishing trawler which fished from here until 1982, when it was taken over by a collector from Inverness.* Myriam isn't pretty, but in this photo she has the air of knowing what she wants. She is wearing a little Hassidic-style skullcap. In the 1960s, the successive queens look like Jean Seberg and then Charlotte Rampling. At least, they did their best. The attendant whom I asked about this dynasty told me, 'In the old days, the most popular and the cleverest were chosen, today it's just the prettiest, who'll make a good marriage later.'

---

* This is the name that NB gives, but in fact the 1952 queen was Margaret Young, with Margaret and Jean Maltman in her train; in 1955 it was Agnes Maltman. (Trs.)

She has every reason to disparage this turn of events, which had cost her a royal position: she is local, very intelligent, and ugly. Under the former criteria she would have been elected and perhaps married. Like Myriam Maltmann, who owns three trawlers today and is indeed the 'Herring Queen'. The attendant, born a little too late, accompanied me to the exit where you can see a big collage made by schoolchildren at the turn of the century. Always the famous wreck: you see the mast of the sailing-ship and, borne on the swell, a vast circle of roughly cut-out little men, holding hands beatifically.

'The survivors?'

'No, those are the dead.'

A narrow ribbon of perfect asphalt snakes its way through the incredible solitude of the moors of Lammermuir. Night is falling. The crossroads have no signposts and the villages pretentiously indicated on the map consist of one, two or three farms which seem to be abandoned. It's Sunday. I keep losing my way. It's all the same to me, I'm used to it: I and my best friends have been lost all over the place. We are lost in this world. I remember a house at a crossroad, with light in one window. A big man in a maroon sweater opens the door, listens to me, and points in the direction of the night. His hand clasps a dart with a green plastic top. Darts and leek competitions are the favourite pastimes of these reclusive, taciturn farmers.

South of St Bathans, just as the sun set, the countryside became splendid. I had been told again and again that the Scottish countryside is one of the most beautiful in the world. I hadn't been told that it is the light and not the geology which does all the work. The geology is the sort found everywhere: a worn crust, rounded or jagged. The light (rapidly changing skies, swift winds, wildly changeable light-levels) is unimaginable and makes more magical images in a day than the eye can take in. And from whatever landscape – ugly, unassuming, common. I've only seen it play so fast and freely with what the planet offers in the east of Iran, or in Java. Now I understand better why the Scots are at once so poetic yet not grandiloquent: they are 'struck' by the light, like punch-drunk boxers.

I was rather struck myself when I stopped the car because the narrow road was entirely covered by a pheasant that had been run over. It had been hit full-on, and exploded like a grenade in a perfect projection. Its intestines, its feathers, the big, striped tail-feathers were spread out on the black surface, stuck down by blood or fresh tar with admirable symmetry, suggesting an Art Deco pattern or those 'works of art' made by diplomats' wives whiling away their time in climates just too cold or just too hot. The softest feathers were still trembling at a breath of wind. I said to myself that a Scot in a kilt, squashed in the same way, would have presented almost the same range of colours. I reversed the car and went through a field rather than spoil such a masterpiece. All the same, I did take a couple of large feathers, a little bit stained, for my calligrapher friends (better than goose-feathers, surely?) and I drove along more slowly than before.

I found both my way and my spirits in the fully licensed bar in Gordon, where no stranger stops and the local youths make an uproar. They were already sozzled and my appearance was greeted with loud whistles, going down a notch when one of the girls pointed out that I was wearing a gold ring in my left ear: a traveller who's made his fortune is pushed around less than a mere outsider. They raised their glasses vaguely in my direction, I did the same, and then each returned to his business, mine being to quench my thirst. Everything got noisier. The bar formed a right angle: the girls were seated along one side, the boys on the other. The handsomest boy was seriously drunk and, as the barman refused to serve him, the most beautiful girl (already past her best, but a real beauty) made a remark about the effect of alcohol on his virility. He got up, went over to her, lifted her off her stool (very gently, as if handling the best china), put her down on the ground and held her in a mock embrace, returned her to her stool in the same old-fashioned manner and returned to his own, saying, 'I could've almost made her do it.' I was waiting for her to slap him, or for someone to intervene.

A second later she joined him, nibbled his ear nicely, took his wallet to save Saturday's pay, and went out. He gazed after her in amazement. Before and during this scene (I was watching them from the time I came in) the young woman's expression hadn't changed in the slightest; it consisted of intelligent compassion, of complicity, and of laziness, too. I wondered what she was thinking, back home, waiting for the return of this handsome hunk whom she had protected from his own stupidity without any humiliation, in fact with a skill and elegance that I thought could only exist on another planet. There was a moment of silence in which everyone must have been saying to themselves, 'What a f—g lucky bastard to have her,' then the noise resumed with renewed vigour. I would have been able to leave without paying for my beer; they had completely forgotten me.

I was a bit put off by the name the 'Abbotsford Arms' – it was too fruity, suggesting a dynasty of wealthy confectioners. Because of the Abbey, which attracts so many visitors, I was afraid of a tourist conspiracy *à la* Saint-Sulpice. But no. Arriving in Melrose beneath a quarter-moon was amazing. You cross the River Tweed over a stone bridge (I had turned the engine off in order not to miss its loud murmur), you make out a mass of foliage swaying a little in the dark and enter the main street which rises gently, lined with old houses sitting side by side in that natural harmony you find in the towns of Burgundy or Franche-Comté. You realise that wherever monks built churches or monasteries, and their work benefited the local economy, secular architecture also profited – from their knowledge of golden rules, balance and standards that produced exemplary, graceful towns. I parked the car opposite the Abbotsford Arms. I was happy to have arrived somewhere, having driven for seven or eight hours (in Scotland, as in Ireland, the roads twist and turn for no other reason, it seems, than to allow you to admire all aspects of the landscape). As I extracted myself from the car, carefully, on account of my sore back, an old man in a cap gestured towards me, grimaced toothlessly in imitation of my curved spine, quavered, 'Too much driving,' and promptly disappeared.

I dined on trout with almonds at a table at the end of the bar, the large tables with their cloths in the dining-room – where I would have been more comfortable sitting and writing – only being available to those wearing jackets and ties. I hadn't brought either with me, but envisaged repairing this omission in order to have the right to a silver salt-cellar, a damask napkin and the conversation of sober people, which is infinitely more interesting than that of drunks (a long acquaintance with alcohol permits me to say this), given that I am an eavesdropper here.

In my room I had a good table with decent lighting. In Scotland I always found, even in the simplest lodgings, the three things I require of a room: a table, even a small one, with a lamp; a wastepaper basket; enough blankets. I poured a good measure of whisky into a tooth-mug (I prefer to buy it from a grocer's than at the bar), unfolded a map, and made a mental inventory of what I knew about Scotland, like a gypsy with his petty hoard. First of all images from the Épinal prints of early childhood, like those the missionaries gave out under the coconut palms to teach piccaninnies the importance of Joan of Arc, Napoleon, Victoria – thus: bagpipes (which can be found as far away as Iran), kilts, tartan, Shetland ponies, the Loch Ness Monster. Not to mention the *fil d'Ecosse* (lisle thread) which made the expensive socks I was given at Christmas or New Year. I would have preferred one of those spinning-tops which hummed and sang but, in Geneva, presents had to be useful and, if possible, last until you died.

Then there was reading. In the early 1930s, without radio or television, we stuffed ourselves with books as no one does these days. Thus, between the ages of eight and twelve: Walter Scott, not all, but five or six novels; R. L. Stevenson a bit later, read and re-read to this day, above all his admirable *On the Art of Writing*. But in that period it was *Treasure Island* or *Dr Jekyll* and I had no idea that Stevenson was Scottish. In all good faith I thought he was a wizard and a pirate, a green parrot on his shoulder, phials of potions or poisons tucked into his broad belt, next to his cutlass. Pirates, like wizards, belong to no country. Then, family history: we didn't move directly from being French Huguenots to Genevans. One of my ancestors had rowed in the same galley as John Knox, who was sentenced to four years of rowing for having killed the Bishop of Edinburgh – along with some 'justified' men of the same persuasion – as revenge for the hanging of a reformist by the same bishop, because the man had read the scriptures in public. I hope that this ancestor, also considered to be an 'ordinary prisoner', had equally honourable motives. Then another, courtier to James II during his French exile, was put to death by Louis XIV, following a conspiracy in which he supplied many barrels of gunpowder. To whom? Why? I haven't the slightest idea. I have a magnificent engraved portrait of this martyr, which the spiders in my attic have turned into an Impressionist canvas. Amen.

Then, during my studies, some names which are blanks on the map because even if I had to know about them I didn't suppose I had to read them: Robert Burns, James Macpherson-Ossian. Besides, I never got an hour's English during my interminable schooldays and brief time at university, only Middle-High German, Latin, Sanscrit: the effect of the dead hand of Saussure. I learnt English much later, in India and Japan, which was perhaps not the best schooling. If my vocabulary is good, my accent makes even a retriever laugh. Let's say no more about it. My knowledge of this country was thus derisory and useless. I knew less about it than about Chinese Turkestan. I was thrilled by this bare ignorance: everything was, everything is, everything must be from now on a lesson, a surprise, a question. I thought of the cry of Jan Hus when he saw a devout peasant add a faggot to the stake at which he and his truth were already beginning to roast: 'O sancta simplicitas!' So help me, God.

I woke up to a fine drizzle, and swore. By the time I was shaving the sun had appeared, slanting between two cushions of cloud. Here you can never trust the weather forecast because the weather changes eleven times a day. Well before I reached the Abbey, towards which I was ambling in no particular hurry, I received the greatest gift the Scottish Borders could offer me: trees. Elms, beeches, ash and plane trees the likes of which one only sees in dreams: majestic, restless, immense, their foliage at its best, just about to turn yellow. The lime trees know all of Schubert by heart. I suspect that people here are almost as in love with botany as people in my city. If you wish to cheer up a Genevan, make him lose his frown and his dry manner, show him a weeping willow or a copper beech. He will forget the rates on the stock exchange and the *bise noire* (north wind) which afflicts us. Around our university most of the streets are named after botanists, and Stendhal noted that Genevan clockmakers spent their days off in botanising. Because of this long-standing hobby, the planting of the Genevan landscape is an enchantment, and I thought it was unique in Europe. I was wrong: it is just as well done here. Not only in the great variety of species, but also in the way they have been planted, which always seems to have been managed by a landscaping genius. For a mind such as mine – dark, anxious, disorganised – the contemplation of trees has always been a powerful comfort. Slowness, balance, murmurs or silence – we die of the absence of these things. I'm going to meander through the Borders in a constant state of dendrological intoxication.

But, you'll say to me, on the sheep hills in the west there are no trees to be seen. Yes and no. There are great, brown stretches of grazing land under wild skies, where the ewes cling on like ants to a cheese rind. There are also, scattered everywhere, hideous recent battalions of spruces, planted solely for the landowner's profit, elbow to elbow like Frederick of Prussia's grey infantry with their green braid: soulless, unsurprising, unimaginative, without squirrels. Besides, no bird would want to nest among them, so monotone, mechanical, basely commercial. But where the bare countryside has been saved from this leprosy you find here and there a bouquet of lonely pines, a solitary oak, and their placement is marvellous, as if Turner or Corot had pointed with his paintbrush to a spot on the horizon saying, 'You will grow there.'

Between Melrose and the amazing Sweetheart Abbey south of Dumfries, you will find half a dozen magnificent monasteries which all appear to have suffered the fate of Coventry under Nazi bombing. That isn't the case: they were built between the tenth and thirteenth centuries, first by monks from Ireland then by Benedictines from Picardy, the 'French connection'. Destroyed by Viking raids, then rebuilt. Destroyed in the course of the Anglo-Scottish wars which bloodied the Borders in the fifteenth century, and rebuilt. Destroyed again in the sixteenth century by the Earl of Hertford, Henry VIII's general, who carried out his mission to the Scots by putting the population to the sword at the least sign of discontent. Then Cromwell, with his stocks of powder and cannon, finally felled what remained of those fine networks of stone desperately reaching up to the heavens.

I don't know why Ireland and Scotland don't have a national annual celebration in common to celebrate the death of Oliver Cromwell. That man destroyed almost as many beautiful things as Genghis Khan. In Ireland, where the historic fabric is less well preserved than here, every time I saw a ruin I was told 'Cromwell'. His rapacity extended to the very rocks. Three years ago, in the south of Galway, I was walking with an archaeologist who showed me an enormous depression in a field beside the road, a negative imprint, grassed over in a semi-circle, and he said: 'There was a stone with an interesting shape there; it was stolen away and only the hole remains.' I asked who had taken it away – the Vikings? (They'd stolen many objects.) No: Cromwell.

Today all the Border abbeys are as ruined as the Coliseum, with two differences: you won't find half-starved cats in them, nor gay prostitutes. Nor will you find Roman decay: the archaeologists have wielded their chisels, their scrapers, their brushes so successfully that all trace of burning and violence has been removed, and the rosy stone has turned pink again, so that it takes a moment to realise that these elegant skeletons were not built like this in the nineteenth century exclusively for Ruskin's delectation. All doubt disappears when you take a close look at the fragments of sculpture preserved in the little museum next to the Abbey. Two examples struck me: a siren and the head of a Moor, which served as gargoyles in the thirteenth and fourteenth centuries. The siren is a true siren, with all the troubling eroticism that her kind has always inspired: her provocative breasts are easily grabbed, but how to penetrate her? The Moor is a true Moor: snub-nosed, patient, haughty. Here we are in the presence of the dynamic imagination of the Middle Ages. Since then, there's been so much bullshit about figurative art that these days no one is capable of making an effigy that those two would recognise.

The Abbey reposed under the drizzle, shining like the carcass of a great Catholic whale washed up on a beach of sparkling, perfect grass. If it had been intact, I might have found something to criticise, some sentimental, late-Gothic notes dating to the final reconstruction. Half-ruined as it is, it escapes all criticism. Who reproaches a whale for having been washed up, for having been picked over by various predators, leaving us this mysterious dictation in bone? A walk in the graveyard, which extends behind the nave. The tombs, as in Turkey, are all askew, and their inscriptions offer all the forms of writing from the Middle Ages to today: Times Roman or Rockwell for the dead of the Dardanelles or Dunkirk, lovely English Romantic for the contemporaries of Walter Scott, Gothic for those tombs which escaped the vandalism of successive conquerors and the hammer of the Protestant iconoclasts.

While the headstones of the departed, encircled by angels' wings, had been eaten away by time, I didn't find anything tragic in the inscriptions I could decipher. As in the *Scotsman's* obituaries, all had died 'peacefully' and effusively eulogised by their survivors. Their relationship with the beyond seems more relaxed than ours. No doubt it is the effect of the lawn, its perfection of colour and texture, which acts on me like opium and whose redemptive green forbids all sentiments of mourning or failure. I should add that you can run across these lawns, or have a nap on them. They are not forbidden to trespassers, as in our strict gardens, nor 'placed under citizens' watch', that is, under the eye of future informers.

I can't walk a hundred metres without my legs seizing up and without sitting down on my providential shooting-stick. However, it isn't pain but the strong smell of mussels (they're delicious here) which causes me to sit down at this table of blackened oak in the Marmion restaurant. *Marmion* is a long epic poem glorifying the British nation (all rivalry forgotten) that Walter Scott published anonymously in 1808 and whose success played a part in reconciling the English and the Scots in the face of the Napoleonic threat.* It's also the name of this bistro, hung with French posters from the 1900s advertising Deauville, *cirages Jacot* (Jacot shoe polish), and Loie Fuller's show. In one corner there's a huge Eiffel Tower, 1930s kitsch. The tables are full of regular customers who seem to think more and speak faster than their fellow natives. Here, the calm beauty of the countryside and the intoxicating theatricality of the weather invite one to dream, 'to be' rather than 'to say or do', to be mentally lazy, and after three days I'm affected in the same way. Compared with the other pubs in town, this place is a friendly hornets' nest. The manager, humming as he comes over to take my order, quickly understands that I'm looking for informants. He seats a young, sturdy redhead – as lively as a weasel – at my table. She's a journalist from London who has lived here for eight years. 'She has an excellent outsider's view of the Borders.'

---

* NB is perhaps relying on a blurred recollection of the poem here. Subtitled 'A Tale of Flodden Field', it takes place around the bloodiest battle fought between Scotland and England, in which the Scottish King James IV was killed – not really the grounds for reconciliation. Also, although Scott at first published his novels anonymously, he was well known as a poet. (Trs.)

She informs me, without once drawing breath, that you have to wait a long time for an 'inside view'. The locals hate talking about themselves, speak as little as possible, and consider even clearing the throat as a sign of excessive vanity. That she works for women's magazines in London, but lives here because her husband deals in tweed and wool as far as Hong Kong and Taiwan, and it's advantageous for him to buy at the source. That she has a dream house on the river, with a ghost who tells her all sorts of funny stories, and she's writing a history of it with her daughter. That she can show me on the map the places where women make tapestries or craft with straw or carve shepherd's crooks. (I know such ladies, scattered across Europe, who punctuate their activities with bouts of hatha yoga or tai chi; they and their weaving don't interest me at all.) That in nearby Jedburgh they make the best bows in Britain. That the quality of life has really improved over the last few years thanks to educated, quiet tourists. That a woman who doesn't hunt or ride spends her life in the kitchen, as the men don't approve of their wives working. That next Friday there would be traditional music in a pub at St Mary's Loch, a hundred kilometres away. That she adores Melrose but goes back to London once a fortnight to live life in the fast lane and sharpen her wits. She added that life here was very provincial and chauvinist, with the lowest rate of crime in Britain; a girl of eleven could walk round the town all night without risking a hair on her head. That there was no unemployment here and that a pony cost less than a bike.

With which she returned to her river, her house and her ghost. God bless her.

Chauvinist: yes. At Selkirk, just near by, they have a saying, 'A day away from Selkirk is a day wasted.' Provincial? It does seem that the sea breeze is much diminished by the time it reaches the little gardens, hollyhocks and espaliers of these happy hobbits. I took the *Border Telegraph* and *Southern Reporter* off the racks. On the former the big headline: 'New bus-stop vandalised'. Reading on, you learn that some rascal who'd had too much to drink had peed on it and left some dubious graffiti on the walls. Oh no! There is none the less a suicide: 'Selkirk stunned by shooting tragedy'. A young businessman, who had swindled an insurance company by burning down one of his factories, had killed himself after shooting his dog.

Of course people can take their own lives in the most peaceful and supportive communities, but really it isn't done here. Moreover, it's a sin in the eyes of John Knox's church, and the neighbours' remarks express more condemnation than compassion: 'It was horrible – like something out of *Miami Vice*.'

I was amused to learn that a miniature train for children, a fairground family's only money-spinner, would be part of the fair at Yarrow and had arrived yesterday, on an enormous truck. And obviously happy to learn that Mrs Sheila Caryl (this notice had top billing) of Kelso would be among the finalists of the women's darts contest in Swinton. Ah! I almost forgot: a parish councillor from J. admitted to having sexual relations with a young Greek woman during an ecumenical congress on the island of Syros. As he had not drawn on the kitty but paid for his distractions entirely out of his own pocket, he retained the 'complete confidence' of the parish council.

Please don't think that I'm making fun of them. The local papers in my country report almost the same stories. They're even more provincial, if that's possible. Perhaps because you wouldn't read the names Syros or Miami in them. Perhaps because, under Calvin, the parish council would not have 'complete confidence' in a repentant fornicator. With a slight gap, our two nations have followed the same route: in a little over a century they have lost their spirit of adventure and have moved from a harsh existence, often as mercenaries (Swiss and Scots plundered the planet and sold their skins almost everywhere, often under the command of swindling colonels who pocketed half their pay), to a pleasant, hushed conformity. Shakespeare gave way to Labiche, tragedies to the niceties of vaudeville. Families behave better. It's regrettable, all the same.

It was not so long ago that these Borderers were rovers and map-makers. It was the Scots who established a whole network of lighthouses around the coast of Japan, after the Meiji restoration. They were famous rustlers, too: they went out on night raids into Northumberland and took sheep back to Scotland along paths known only to the Scots. These pilferers were known as 'rievers'. At the beginning of the eighteenth century it was said that the most famous of them would find 'a dish of spurs' instead of soup at his place, to remind him that his wife and sons thought he'd had sufficient rest and that there were still too many sheep on the other side of the border. These ancient exploits are celebrated in summer by the 'common ridings', when people spend whole days riding the boundaries of their towns. A town of three thousand inhabitants can easily muster five hundred riders – men, women, children and the elderly all mixed in. Cups are drained at all the inns along the route. It's a commemoration: the epic spirit of yesteryear has been altogether lost.

So let's turn elsewhere – and to the olden days!

I don't like visiting castles at all, but a visit to the manor that Sir Walter Scott built on the site of a farm where he spent his childhood is not to be missed. You enter the park through a modest postern, and in this afternoon's rain the French-style garden with its lawns and bowling-greens is sumptuously melancholy. We'll pass by the neo-Gothic building, but the landscape around it has that velvet quality so often found in the Borders. On a table on the terrace there's a teapot and two cups (the sugar-bowl has been taken in because of the downpour). Descendants of Scott still live here, and visitors' money supports the upkeep of the house and grounds.* They have their own quarters and the continual stream of visitors doesn't disturb them at all.

But best of all there is an old guide, whose grey uniform with brass buttons is provided by the family and whose name might as well be Scheherazade. We are in the bedroom where Scott departed from this deceiving world, his eyes fixed on the loop of the River Tweed which flows through the far end of the grounds. 'We' are a primary-school class with its two teachers. Tiny red-headed girls and boys who don't know much about life are hanging on the guide's every word. Me too: his talk is spellbinding. I have the impression that he makes it up to suit his audience and I'm convinced that he never gives the same one twice. His English is magnificent; he doesn't dumb-down for the kids but when a word or a name needs explaining, he does so in a clear and simple way. He literally trembles

---

* Patricia Maxwell-Scott – Sir Walter's great-great-great-granddaughter – died in 1998 and her sister, Dame Jean Maxwell-Scott, inherited Abbotsford. She kept it going as a visitor attraction until her death in 2004, when a trust was established to look after the estate. (Trs.)

with admiration for the dead man whom he brings to life cleverly, with small touches, by means of each object he chooses. Here are the tiny spectacles of the good giant; the built-up shoes which he wore to offset the limp resulting from childhood polio; the desks and the decanters given by Goethe and Byron; the armour, the Roman coins, the books of spells that this collector saved from obscurity and which contributed to his writing of the history of Scotland. The last letter he wrote to his French wife, whom he adored. A casket made of wood from the wreck of the Spanish Armada.

No article in this little museum is uninteresting, and each plays a part in piecing together the figure of a man whom Scotland has literally canonised. For excellent reasons. I am suspicious of excessive virtue, which is usually incompatible with the lack of restraint which governs all true creation. An exception must be made for Scott. I know that I won't re-read the books from my childhood: life is too short to go back to *Ivanhoe* or *Rob Roy* – anyway, I remember them very clearly because early memories, as has been shown, are those that last longest. Whatever the historical and political importance of his *oeuvre*, his character interests me much more now than his books. Besides, why did French publishers at the beginning of the twentieth century put authors as important as Scott, Stevenson and Jack London in the category of children's books? Because, entirely taken up with the fashion for psychological novels and pure belles-lettres, they regarded the adventure story as a childish genre. Thanks to them, while still in short trousers I was able to read excellent (sometimes terrifying) writers without any family disapproval.

A word, then – setting literary criticism aside – on the man who was so engaging. Walter Scott was the son of a Kelso lawyer. He was a man of the Borders. From his cradle he was rocked to dark tales of the last Scottish defeats, in which a good part of his clan had been killed. An illness from which he recovered made of him, from the age of six, a guzzler of books – like Montaigne, of whom he reminds me in more than one respect. Aged twelve, he was registered at the University of Edinburgh where, as well as the law, he learnt four or five languages. Aged twenty-one he was called to the bar, and began to translate Goethe. Seven years later he was Sheriff-Depute of Selkirk, and soon to publish (anonymously, since a Crown magistrate could not be a novelist or a poet) his first writings, which were immensely successful. He married the daughter of a refugee from the French Revolution, who was the love of his life. He adored his family (four children), who returned his affection. His affable character was so charismatic that the farmyard animals followed him as they followed Orpheus; one little piglet was so enchanted by him that he followed at his heels and slept under his desk, squealing with pleasure, as Scott wrote.

When he acknowledged authorship of his bestsellers, *Waverley* was printed in fabulous quantities, and he became the most celebrated author in Britain and corresponded with all the great men on the Continent. His credit in London allowed him to obtain many advantages for his native land, notably the Scottish banks' right to continue printing their own banknotes. One more piece of evidence of his astonishing character concerned the French prisoners who, after Waterloo, had been placed under the surveillance of the inhabitants of Selkirk. If we are to believe *Highways and Byways in the Border* by Andrew and John Lang, published in the early twentieth century, their captivity was very well spent because the Scots, although detesting Napoleon, had remained Francophile at bottom. They were amused by the way their 'prisoners' ate the frogs from local ponds, and were happy to turn a blind eye when they saw them move, little by little, the notice-post which marked the limit fixed for their walks. Scott, who was a sheriff after all and bound to uphold the law, collected the most literate prisoners in a closed carriage and conveyed them to Abbotsford for secret suppers, which the Marquis Doisy de Villargennes held in fond memory.

Walter Scott didn't understand money. At the peak of his fame he went bankrupt, along with his friend and associate Ballantyne. Abbotsford had cost him a fortune; he owed over a hundred thousand pounds to his creditors. Right up to his death he would allocate all his author's rights to reimbursing them down to the last penny.

One might be surprised that a man as skilled at happiness could have written novels as sinister as *The Bride of Lammermoor* (Lammermuir on the map). Perhaps he purged himself of the tragedy inherent in life through his writings. One thing is certain: Walter Scott worked hard to establish the identity of Scotland that the severe guardianship of England and the country's own internecine quarrels had obscured. One could apply to this catalyser of national energies the fine lines he himself wrote:

Come one, come all! This rock shall fly
From its firm base as soon as I.

Selkirk. The Scots are in love with their past and revive it very cleverly and tastefully. Here, a large grocery-hardware store, which had been in the same family for six or seven generations and fallen into disrepair, was bought up by the municipality and very carefully restored to the exact form it would have had in 1880, to serve as a witness to the everyday life of the period. I say 'witness' and not 'museum' because there are several examples of each article, many as good as new, labelled with the prices taken from catalogues or advertisements of the time. With the wave of a magic wand, the gilded cast-iron cash-register would be able to work again. All the fittings were still there, from the long, polished oak counter to the chests whose drawers bear white enamel knobs with blue letters, like the stops on an old-fashioned harmonium. As for the objects, happily the citizens of Selkirk are hoarders and only had to raid their attics for the necessary merchandise. Here you find: oil-lamps, candle-snuffers, tinder-boxes, irons to be heated on the stove, copper warming-pans for heating chilly beds, tallow candles, sulphur matches to strike on the sole, demi-johns of thick blue glass full of bubbles in wicker casing, blocks of sugar in strong brown paper, liquorice, mints, mustard poultices, and a whole range of infusions to repair failing hearts and reduce swollen legs.

As I was making an inventory of these marvels, a group of Canadian visitors came in. After a brief pause, the two eldest members, convinced they were in a real shop, insisted to the attendant that they would buy some of the things which reminded them of their youth. They came from Mackenzie where the grocers' shops, before the Second World War, were almost exactly the same as this one.

Pub in Galashiels. I observe my neighbours and shortly attempt a typology of the Border Scot – like a naturalist seeing a pterodactyl flying past in the autumn – and come up with this: first, usually not very tall, the broad torso slightly curved as though to resist the wind, which he will have to do all his life. Lively eyes, sometimes lost in thought, slightly long-sighted and somewhat given to hallucinations. Often with the look of someone who widens their eyes in order to detect a sheep in fog, or a boat stranded on a reef. Both men and women seem to be firmly established in this deceptive world, have a no-nonsense air, as if Thomas Aquinas's adversary John Duns Scotus (1266–1308), whom three towns here claim as their son, had personally convinced each of them of the excellence of the 'reality principle'. The bearing, too, of people who, despite being victims of abuses, violence and appropriations, live within the fabric of an ancient culture, dense and continuous – different in this way from Ireland where, after the flowering of the early Middle Ages to which Christian Europe owes so much, everything fell back into a sort of night. The Lowlands are not the Boglands.

Yesterday, in a piece about Scott, I came across the words 'moss-trooping riders', which intrigued and pleased me. Did it refer to the famous cattle-thieves? Did they pass through mossy forests like the Louisiana bayous with their booty? I asked my friends at the Marmion, who didn't know, but assured me that it had nothing to do with actual moss, and that it was probably a term from the secret geography of the Borders.

This evening at the Town Arms Inn, which is a bit less hushed than mine, the barman said to me, 'If you just want to taste the ice, why such a good whisky?' I learnt to drink it, after thirty years, the proper way: without water or ice, in small sips, making it last. Although it isn't expensive here, people don't get drunk on whisky: it's too good. At the next table, two young actors, bearded natives, were working on a play by Synge with a very commanding woman who seemed to be their teacher. Each word she spoke reached everyone in the room, which people here absolutely hate. She had a bold, greedy, haggard face, but a very pretty body, with perfect breasts in which she took some pride. She should have worn them like carnations where her face was, and tucked away that clashing sight under her blouse. I would thus have had an erotic, amusing, Max Ernst-style figure opposite me; perhaps her conversation would have been engaging. She was from Los Angeles (as everyone could tell) and here to run an acting course. I asked her two sidekicks what 'moss-trooping riders' meant. They hadn't a clue. For her part, she had an explanation so ridiculous that I immediately forgot it. She shouted to the company at large, 'But don't quote me,' and burst into a crazy laugh that was far too loud.

An old man who was drinking alone in his corner then came up to me, politely touched his finger to his cap, sat down and explained the true meaning. These 'moss-trooping riders' were the children of men killed at the battle of Culloden who, some months or years afterwards, attacked a squad of cavalry without warning, to avenge their dead. Eighty set out and seventeen returned, with the flag taken from their enemy. This childish and mortal ambush had taken place at Moss-paw.* I believe this was the last bloody conflict between the two nations. After Bannockburn (1314), when the King of Scotland roasted the English, the Scots lost almost all the great battles, though won many skirmishes, of which this was the last. They lost not for lack of valour – their nerve is legendary – but sometimes through lack of artillery, and always through lack of unity. The clans took far too long to understand that they couldn't outface the English while they were fighting amongst themselves. Once or twice they lost through a kind of poetic, pre-Romantic, poignant absent-mindedness. In 1174 William the Lion, King of Scotland, charged the English army at the head of his cavalry (up to the fifteenth century it was the Scots who initiated the fighting). He was so intent on the matter in hand and on his fame, and the hoofs of his charger made such a noise, that he didn't notice that none of his men were behind him. Arriving alone at the English lines, he was plucked like a ripe plum, with a mixture of hilarity and respect. Having surrendered his sword, he went back, and through several layers of mist heard the laughter of the men who hadn't followed him. It's a story about clan loyalties again, although Scottish historians refuse to be clear about this. What they do have

---

* This is probably a story. The 'moss-trooping riders' were like the Border rievers but active in the mid-seventeenth century, and acts were passed against their activities in 1662 and 1666. Culloden (1746) was the last battle of the failed Jacobite uprising of 1745. (Trs.)

to recognise is that to win his freedom, this solitary rider had to cede the rich town of Berwick to the English.

Dined with Michael Ambrose, a friend of the Marmion's proprietor, who made me taste – along with excellent beer – Scotland's national dish, haggis: sheep's intestines minced with barley, and mashed turnips. The taste wasn't as bad as I'd been told; indeed, it was a savoury dish. What you have to contend with is the smell of manure that rises from the plate, strong and distracting. In his office I saw a postcard with an intensely blue loch set amidst bare green hills. I had seen enough of these little dolled-up towns and visited enough gingerbread abbeys. I looked at the road map: there was an inn at each end of the loch. Decided to go and sleep in that spot, passing by Traquair, the oldest continuously inhabited house in Scotland. Travelling west to Innerleithen, the Tweed runs on your left scarcely fifty metres below the road, meandering slow and clear in the dip between cropped grass or willows and gorse. Sheep are balled together like white pinheads against the green of the fields. Mellow light. On this journey I couldn't walk as I really like doing – or could hardly walk – or take advantage of such wagons, buses or little trains that happened along. Thus I had to stop the car a dozen times over less than sixty kilometres to let this healing view do its work. And in terms of scenery, I hadn't seen anything yet.

Traquair House (late afternoon). A tall, severe façade made of even-sized dressed stones the colour of whitened bones. Narrow windows suggest interminable winters. Traquair recalls certain châteaux in Périgord or Limousin: a brutalist architecture that is very subtly balanced. I sit down on the slippery parquet to rest my legs in a little salon where all the chairs have silken cords roping them off, or wires attached to the alarm system. Lifting my head, I see through the window the edge of a huge park, where several peacocks parade in front of wrought-iron gates, closed – they say – since the defeat of the last Stuart. It was vowed they would not be opened until the Stuarts regained the throne of Scotland, which is to say never. A more local version, which I prefer, speaks of a mistress stolen along with some of the family silver, long awaited, gates closed, divided between hope and disappointment. It doesn't matter.

The wall facing me is covered with ancient maps depicting the vast Ettrick forest (each tree is drawn), cut down in the nineteenth century for Nelson's navy and today grazed by sheep, and, on the heavy dressers, the china services brought by the clippers which sailed on the tea run between Canton and the mouth of the Thames. On one plate I see a mandarin slide his long sleeve under a courtesan's skirt: the three strands of his beard shine with mischief in the twilight. I walk alone from room to room and floor to floor, accompanied by a commentary recorded by the master of the place, which comes on automatically as you cross the threshold. After politely bidding me welcome, my invisible host (a Stuart) offered detailed information about the nicknames, habits and whims of the numerous ghosts with whom he shares the house.

He didn't mention that of Mary Stuart, who spent several nights of her erratic life here; however a whole room is devoted to her. Coloured lithographs from the early nineteenth century – it is this romantic iconography that has made of the queen a murdered, silly turtle-dove, victim of the fickle nobles: the slender white neck, eyes lifted to the heavens, the axe with its huge, shining blade! Whereas the woman was actually muddled, somewhat naïve and limited, and extremely athletic; she galloped nearly a hundred miles in two days to see Bothwell in his Hermitage Castle, an exploit most riders would not be capable of, and, indeed, afterwards she fell ill. She was only occasionally able to understand what was really at stake. Entangled with the wretched Darnley, who was wracked by conceit and jealousy, she was disliked by her subjects. Disentangled herself so clumsily! I am convinced that with a slightly more politic head screwed on, she would have been able to conclude a sort of 'edict of Nantes' with John Knox who, despite his ferocious misogyny, was more of a patriot and a Scot than a fanatic.*

Two hours later I arrived at the Mountbenger Inn, and after much confusion and muddle I was able to obtain the last vacant room, in which the bed was as damp as a layer of mushrooms. Then I was seated opposite an old man who had come every year for thirty years to fish in the Yarrow. He explained to me that the permit was cheaper than that for the Tweed, although the fish were exactly the same. And what did he fish? Salmon trout and sea trout.

---

* The Edict of Nantes was signed in 1598 by Henry IV of France, an essentially Catholic nation, giving rights to French Protestants. (Trs.)

I went out for a breath of air – the sky was glorious, which promised well for the next day, and in the dark I heard the swift flowing river descending to St Mary's Loch. All the immense surrounding countryside of trout and sheep belongs to the Duke of Buccleuch, the largest private landowner in Scotland. Even in the dark I could tell that this county was indescribably beautiful. Returning to the pub, I was all the more struck by the indescribable ugliness of everything in it: saffron-yellow formica tables, as unfortunate in the daylight as at night. On the walls, garish pictures of bulldogs in waistcoats playing billiards, and two blurred charcoal drawings of huge sheepdogs, with bewhiskered muzzles like Clemenceau; they were the owner's dogs and the living models were right in front of me: the mother asleep on her back, teats in the air, softly moaning in the grip of a juicy dream. The daughter had decided to place her heavy jaw on my thigh and wouldn't be dislodged. All right – I'm not a man for dogs but I like the large, sleepy, fluffy kind. The owner's daughter came to my table to salute my patience and offered me a malt whisky. Her father, slow and resigned (to what?), was obviously letting his life and his inn fall apart.

She was studying political economy at the University of Glasgow and wasn't letting go of anything. I saw the procession of her suitors come in the back door one by one, have a beer and then depart. She wanted to talk about the Continent, but we ended up talking about the place itself. Listening to her, it seemed that this Duke of Buccleuch was considered a good landlord, but a stickler for maintaining the dry-stone walls which ran for miles sometimes, demarcating the huge grazing grounds which anyway all belonged to him. One breech, one loose stone, and there was trouble. Why? I would soon learn that the life of a white, black-faced sheep, who is a mountain creature and survives extreme cold, has really nothing to do with the poetry of Virgil or Ovid, but comes straight out of a tale told by a crazy Orwell. She also told me that this Duke, like many landowners, was relentlessly planting trees on his hills, despite the protests of his shepherds, who are not at all beggars in rags but stony-eyed capitalists who keep saying, 'There's no meat in trees.' On which note, I went to bed.

I would almost like to stop this little educational run here. 'Run', yes: I haven't stopped running. 'Educational', yes: I've never stopped, will never stop, learning. I'll die of it. I can't absolutely swear that this is one of the three most beautiful roads in the world. I can say that this road, between Cappercleuch and Tweedsmuir, is one of the most beautiful roads I have travelled in my crazy life. And I have travelled enough for them to be like a ball of golden thread in my mind.

Would you like another one? The road between Moudon and Yverdon via Donneloye, in the Swiss canton of Vaud, because of the perfect way the huge farmhouses with red roofs are set in the hollows and curves of the hills, sometimes amidst pastures, sometimes in forests of beeches mixed with firs. And another one? The one linking Turfan in Chinese Turkestan with the Buddhist monastery of Bezeklik, abandoned in the sands for a thousand years, crossing the Flaming Mountains which are just gullies and trenches in the rock or nipples of sand, in all the shades from pink to crimson covered by the word 'red' since it was invented.

The road which climbs from Cappercleuch to the Megget Reservoir then drops down to the Talla Reservoir is a cantata for four voices: water, hills, clouds and the narrow, shining ribbon of road which climbs and descends, at incredible angles, a succession of humpbacks and little passes. It is just wide enough for one car, only occasionally offering a passing place. But there's nobody else around on this splendid morning, and the saturated hills breathe and hiss and rise to touch the pale yellow clouds rushing through the blue sky. The hills are emerald green, flecked with saffron and bright brown, like a plane-tree leaf beginning to yellow. No sign of any housing in this vast space, but sheep by the thousands, scattered across such huge slopes that they look like sleet caught in sunlight rather than real animals. Driving for a long time, carefully (if you leave the road, your wheels are sucked halfway into the spongy verges), without meeting another living soul, I am intoxicated by this Apollonian spectacle.

Then, widening my eyes, I discovered the minute red mark of a shepherd, no bigger than a lower-case i, miles above the road. I got out my binoculars and leaned against the bank: it was his scarf that was red. I saw him squat down, cupping his hands to make the sound reach his dog, whose spine rippled as he speedily wound between the sheep and called out in his dog language. A few seconds later, I heard the 'Kr-chet-tiiit' and 'Do-doo-dat'. A moment afterwards, lovely funereal music rose from the car (I had left the radio on), a cloud hid the sun and, in the blink of an eye, this vast countryside became deathly. With unimaginable suddenness and violence. I saw the shepherd caught in an uncompleted gesture, like a pillar of salt. The dog, coiled up, was no more than a lifeless ball of hair. For thirty miles around sheep were lying on the slopes, their legs already rigid. Out of the corner of my eye I saw the rusting carcass of my new car, pushed aside to clear the road. The same unearthly music continued to issue forth, and the sky was a huge bowl of smoky crystal. This retinal image lasted about twenty seconds, then the sun came out and everything resumed moving and the appearance of reality.

Other landscapes have played a similar trick on me. Once when I was walking along the verge of a half-dry river south of Isfahan; another time in a twilit wasteland suburb of Nagoya, still pockmarked with bomb craters full to the brim with June rain, where a solitary young woman naked to the waist was doing motocross. I took to my heels, but that was a long time ago. Not this time: today I know that some 'places' (the Bretons say *ker*), either exceptionally hideous or splendid and where man is almost absent, fool us like smoke and mirrors, steal from our hearts a latent image and enlarge it like a gigantic magnifier. It's true to say that on entering this deserted, indescribable region – I hadn't seen anything as beautiful in a long time – I had thought of death at the same time as reflecting how miraculous it was to be alive there, precisely there.

I returned to the car at 11.59. At midday, the music which had accompanied this strange trip stopped. It was Sibelius's Symphony no. 1. Through an amphitheatre of rounded mountains, from here on silent and swollen like risen loaves of bread, I descended towards the Talla Reservoir.

On the empty road leading towards the source of the Tweed, you will see a red and green sign announcing 'Local Museum' and 'Border Collies: training demonstration every day at 12 o'clock'. You stop, you look around: on the right, overhanging the road, there is a tiny log cabin which couldn't possibly be a museum – or if it is, the smallest on the planet, and for that reason worth a visit, even if there's nothing inside. On the left, a rough stone path goes down to a farm flanked by a sheepfold and kennels, facing a field bordered by the Tweed, which runs slowly northwards to a pool just a few kilometres from its source. The situation is wonderful: the landscape would be, too, if it weren't for the controversial tree nurseries on the hills, which make an ugly patchwork of comic-book greenish-blue. One expects to find singular people in such a place, and they are: two are already on the doorstep. It is so isolated here that the noise of an engine brings them out like crickets to the edge of their holes. The man is large, stooped, his ageless face mischievous and weather-beaten; his shapeless felt hat, his hunting-jacket and boots are easier to date – fifteen or sixteen years old. The woman, too: a redhead with green eyes, thin and athletic, with a cloud of curls. Let's say thirty-three.

They asked me in for a moment to sign the visitors' book, where I saw that lots of visitors were from Australia and New Zealand. She comes from Wyoming and he from Newcastle. I suspect that both of them have drafts of theses on Althusser or Walter Benjamin tucked away in a drawer. They knew how to make a better life for themselves. They had met in this deserted region in the era of green dreams, got married and, after a long and hard apprenticeship, had become professional shepherds. It's a very demanding and respected trade here. All year long one shepherd, with the help of three dogs, 'controls' one thousand two hundred to one thousand six hundred sheep, which graze over thousands of hectares. They don't have company except at shearing time and for the disinfectant dip, which the whole herd goes through three times in the summer months, to kill the lice and especially the blue flies which lay their larvae under the animals' mucky tails; without this shampooing in sulphur and soda, the sheep's backsides would end up being eaten. While two men steer the sheep towards the dip, a third mounted on a stepladder grabs them by the neck with a forked stick and plunges their heads into the liquid. If the immersion isn't total, it doesn't work.

The remainder of the year they live by themselves. Today the weather is clear and fresh and from here there isn't a single plume of smoke as far as the eye can see; the first pub I found on my climb is over twenty kilometres away. Since they had feathered their nest and bought this place, a few hectares of land, and left their former trade to become dog trainers, they have visitors more often: classes from the school at Moffat and breeders from all over the world come here to see them work their pupils. These are medium-sized, trim dogs, with short black or light grey hair, who swirl, spin and ripple at the heels of sheep whose obstinacy and stupidity are unequalled.

'The dogs have to be real good, because those sheep are not that clever,' the man remarks to me as we watch them at work. 'Not that clever' is Scottish understatement. The sheep are from the black-faced mountain breed which spend all winter outdoors, the 'silly sheep' of Burns's poem. Heavy, stubborn eyes, aquiline muzzle, a skull that seems to be held together by a headband, reminiscent of the engravings in Lavater's *Physiognomie*: a man-sheep's profile suggesting the irremediable and total absence of any initiative or perception. You guess that if these animals, who don't move unless someone nibbles at their shins or a tuft of broom beckons them, made the effort to say to themselves 'sheep... ewe' their brain would escape in a puff of smoke from the narrow lodging that heaven has given it.

The wife showed me round her 'museum', which in the old days was a schoolroom for a dozen boys who came from galactically distant farms, and today is no more than a nice, straightforward tourist trap. There's nothing to see except some drawings by those boys, who must be pushing fifty by now; some yellowing photos of those artists in smocks, surrounding a teacher long since dead; some wooden desks with initials carved into them such as you see all over the world, wherever there is a blackboard; and some 'traditional' shepherd's crooks, nicely carved out of hazel wood, with motifs among which I believe I saw Mickey and Minnie. Her favourite bitch followed at our heels, lively, more intelligent than the two of us combined, madly eager for compliments. At lambing time these shepherds trot more than a hundred kilometres a day, moving from one expectant ewe to the next to make sure that everything is going well because, since the reafforestation, foxes have returned to the hills.

She only breeds short-haired collies because the other kind, Bearded Collies which look like French Briards or Hungarian Pulis, gather so much ice on their fur during the snow season – from December to March – that they become heavy, falter under the weight they're not able to shake off, and sometimes die of exhaustion. While talking, she never stopped raking her hand through her huge halo of curls, lifting the rebellious ones falling across her eyes. I wondered how she, who also covered a lot of ground, managed in the winter with such a mop of hair. She showed me a book, now out of print, which is her autobiography: *Shepherd's Wife*. In a full-page colour photograph she's shown making the acquaintance of a young bitch already overcome with gratitude. The caption is: 'At last she licked my face. Wow!'

The Eskdalemuir Road. Between Peebles (north), Moffat (west), Dumfries (south) and Hawick (east), the country forms a magic square, or rather diamond, each side no longer than eighty kilometres. In this quadrilateral the space is so oddly modelled and spread out, and the population so scattered, that there's a sense of solitude and emptiness that I hadn't experienced since Lapland or eastern Iran. Of solitude, but by no means of desolation, because the rare farms you glimpse along the narrow road, and the even rarer inns, are miraculously placed in the hollows of shaven hills, seductive and mysterious, almost always cupped by the bend of a river or stream. Coming from the east, I regained the valley of the Ettrick which I followed to its source, and then I pursued the course of the Esk as it descended southwards. Three hours of driving, without coming across a grocer's or a petrol pump.

I wanted to spend the night at the Tibetan monastery of Samye Ling, just before the hamlet of Eskdalemuir, the only place in this valley where you can find a bed, or perhaps a wooden platform and a yak-wool blanket. It was about twenty years ago that two lamas, chased out of their country by the Communist invasion, came to this wild spot – thinking it suitable for meditation – and founded a community which is very active today. It wasn't about making money by selling cheap mantras to Westerners panicked by the idea of death, but about transmitting and teaching a knowledge acquired at a high price and which they judged, quite rightly, to be endangered. The history of Tibetan thought and the particular form of Buddhism it engendered has always swung like a pendulum from missionary endeavour to the most radical withdrawal. On the one hand there was the conversion of Mongolia and the sending of lama-magicians to seduce the Yuan dynasty; on the other, they closed the icy passes, who knows why, and the Potala Palace again became a mythic place and less accessible than the South Pole. Expansion and retraction, like Eddington's star. Before the Maoist invasion, Tibet was forbidden even to the best Western Buddhist scholars. Since his exile, the Dalai Lama has become open and proselytises, no doubt to our benefit.

Anyway the centre here has found sufficient response and support in the West to construct a large building which is a replica (on a reduced scale) of one of the great Lhasa monasteries. I arrived at night. I saw the curved roofs, covered with new, varnished tiles, emerge from a dark grove of pines. Around the windows, the porches, on the entablatures and spacers, the traditional colours of Tibet (three degrees of red, green, blue) struggled feebly against the darkness. I parked the car silently and tiptoed round to the living quarters. The night-watchman had gathered the community where it was warm. On my knees in a flower-bed, peering between the curtains of one of the few lighted rooms, I saw a wan individual, ageless and sexless, head shaved, pudgy in the yellow monk's robe (yes, it was a young Westerner), sitting in the lotus position, speaking calmly to two half-starved girls, grubby and shaking, covered in an incredible number of rings and punk charms. The face of the woman in yellow had the good-natured placidity of one who has passed through fire, and her gaze was lit up with mischievous sparks. The two girls were listening to her with a mixture of fear and relief, as if they had finally arrived somewhere after having long ceased to believe they would.

I couldn't understand anything; I saw lips moving but I wasn't seen or heard. If I had rapped on the windowpane, they would have opened it without any fear and offered me a bed without any fuss. But it was doubtless best for this interview to proceed without interruption. And then I'd have to explain myself and this evening, after this theatre without voices but not without beauty, it was just a bit beyond me. I returned like an Indian scout to the car and drove back down the Ettrick valley, following the noise of the river in the blackest darkness, without meeting anyone.

Buccleuch. By about nine o'clock I was running low on petrol, and considered myself lucky to find a room in the place I'd glimpsed, well down below the road, when going past in the afternoon.

I ate some mussels with French fries in the dimly lit saloon bar, back turned on a huge pool-table where three couples were playing, their laughter high-pitched and loud, as though the inn belonged to them. The women, absurdly made-up for such an out-of-the-way place, pocketed their balls, fags in their mouths. The owner and his wife, who seemed to know them well, greeted each win with smarmy compliments. After a bit they came to my table with a bottle and three goblets. They seemed more fragile than the glass. I said, 'A nice place you have here,' meaning, 'The natural surroundings are enchanting.' She leaned towards me and whispered in my ear, 'They kill me – this whole damn business is killing, simply killing,' and disappeared into the kitchen, dabbing her eyes with her white apron. He remained. He told me he'd been trying to put the place back on its feet for several months, without success, and that his wife couldn't stand it any more. Then, I don't know why, he talked about the death of the poet Robert Burns (that colossal genius whose eyes shone with drink) in the doll's house that the Customs administration, by whom he was employed, had offered him in Dumfries as a mark of their esteem. As he spoke, big tears rolled down his cheeks. I know that Burns makes the whole of Scotland cry, but there was something more going on here. I instinctively touched the back of his hand with my fingertip; he clasped mine and held it between his enormous paws for the time it took to swallow back something rising in his throat. What was he struggling against? I remembered the unexpected scene from several hours earlier: those two lost and frantic girls, their hair crested with red, opposite the unsightly woman calmly making an effort to set them back on their feet. Precarious, flawed little lives beneath the sky, a glittering sky tonight: theirs, hers, mine too. All looking, with what help we could find, for an honourable way out. *So it goes.*

Robert Burns (1759–96), who was at once madly in love with sounds, senses, smells, signs… and cyclically depressed, had also sought his way out. It's why the Scots love him so much. But they love him even more for something else: before he left, he had to arrive. Son of a smallholder always threatened by bailiffs and bankruptcy, his back and his nerves broken as a boy by crushing labour, he did not pursue his schooling and was practically self-educated. Yet he brought into being an *oeuvre* that the whole of Britain hailed as the work of a genius. From Byron to Scott to Carlyle, the praises rained down like meteors.

I saw his tiny cottage in a lane in Dumfries. It's most impressive. You are scarcely inside when a thin old man in a grey shirt springs up and shouts, 'You're most welcome, ma'am, sir – anything you'd like to know?' It's as though he guards the flame of both St Patrick and Duncan, it's like Paul Klee's *Twittering Machine*, his shrill babbling following you from room to room. And it is the home of a cult: the bed where he died, the kitchen table, the desk (worn, pleasing, modest) where the great man wrote are all covered with rosebuds, wild roses, the dried heads of blue thistles, left by his admirers, who come as much from the common people who read him as from the gentry. One sees all the familiar objects which suggest that, even for a man in debt, life was fine and well made (this is perhaps not the accepted view, but it is the impression one gets). You see, for example, the toddy ladles, frail demoiselles, made from bone and burnished silver, with which he measured out his pleasure and his wife's (her ladle is a bit smaller but both have his initials).

You can also see in a case a love letter to one of his many muses, Peggy Chalmers, which says: ...*when I think I have met with you and have lived more of real life with you in eight days than I can do with almost anybody I meet with in eight years...* I don't know whether this brief felicity was renewed. I believe that many fashionable ladies were mocked by Burns, all the while flattering themselves on having 'had' this rustic genius. I think that Peggy Chalmers must have disappeared as quickly from the constellation as so many planets in which we have passionately believed.* No matter. I was dreaming thus when I suddenly found myself at liberty: giving me a little, friendly tap on the head, the nostalgic attendant had gone off to bed.

I did the same, and opened the window: the river was murmuring under a crescent moon. Wild rabbits were running about at top speed. Wow!

---

* Margaret (Peggy) Chalmers (1763–1843), daughter of a farmer, spent eight days with Burns in 1787 on his third Highland tour. Years later she told Thomas Campbell that Burns had proposed to her, but she had refused him. They continued to correspond until her marriage to a banker in December 1788. The letter NB quotes is dated 16 September 1788. (Trs.)

Buccleuch. In the early hours of the morning I sat bolt upright out of a delightful dream in which everything encouraged me to feel revivified and to cast off care. The inn slept on in its unhappiness. I went out and I saw:

The horses shivering and
farting in the field
a defiant rabbit
a blade of grass like a toothpick
at the corner of the rogue's mouth.
He knows everything about me that
I struggle to forget.
In my bones, the weight of many years
in my eyes, the green of the river
and of the hills
which roll along without saying a word.

In the Mists of the
Whisky Isle

Bouvier and his wife visited Islay in August 1990 when he was commissioned to write an article by Géo. *We had corresponded when I was translating* Le Poisson-Scorpion, *and we met in Glasgow for the first time. Although distracted by the loss of a suitcase, he was taken with the sight of a military pipe band marching through George Square. There were lots of mothers and small children watching the parade; Bouvier noted that the pushchairs had transparent rain-covers, which could be 'fastened into place like the cockpit of a Phantom fighter'. This detail did not appear in the published article, nor Bouvier's remark that he had not seen anything like this 'sensible equipment' elsewhere in Europe, but that it was obviously an indication of the weather they could expect. After they had been to the agricultural show on Islay, Bouvier wrote: 'Back in Port Askaig I watched the BBC news. The invasion of Kuwait was still the first item. I saw Caspar Weinberger... a dozen sheep... Saddam Hussein... three prize-winning heifers... Liverpool on the brink of economic collapse... a flock of seagulls in a sunny field. From then until our departure, we didn't see the sun again.'*

Beyond Glasgow the road, glistening with rain, twists as it follows the south shore of Loch Lomond. I was tired of driving and pitching my car into the roadside ferns every time we encountered one of the ten-ton tankers, hooting like a tugboat, carrying whisky from Islay (said to be the best in Scotland). That reminded me of the bottle I had in the boot; I stopped the car at a lay-by. As I was taking a mouthful without my lips touching the bottle, a road-mender emerged from a ditch and stopped beside me. I wiped the top and held out the bottle; I saw his Adam's apple move up and down twice and took back the bottle half-empty. He moved off into the ground-mist, enveloped in a tall column of midges.

A hundred miles from Glasgow, facing the north Atlantic, there's a small, poorly heated pub at Kennacraig, close to the ferry terminal, where people gather to wait for the boat to Islay (pronounced Ai-la), the southernmost island in the Hebrides. From all these cold people in boots, oilskins, thick twill, lodens, soaked woollen hats pulled low across the forehead – the steam rises as from wet dish-towels. They are here, however, for pleasure. About half are stock-breeders on their way to Islay for the agricultural show on 9 August. The other half are birdwatchers, the wives of birdwatchers and the children of birdwatchers, whose chief accessory is an enormous pair of binoculars and whose chief utterance is 'Ssh!'

For you don't visit this island so much to meet the four or five Hebridean types who make up a steeply declining population (about fourteen thousand in 1830 and under four thousand today) as to admire a dozen varieties of ewes, Himalayan goats, heifers, bull calves, foals and ponies; and even more, over a hundred species of birds, especially the migrants. Coming from the north, they settle in Islay from October to May and nest in the peat bogs, to the great joy of ecologists and to the great dismay of the farmers and distillers who use that same peat. Until recently, the arrival of these birds – the white-fronted Greenland goose and the Barnacle goose – rekindled the quarrel between two clans who, forgetting British politeness, were on the point of coming to blows. But not today: this migratory population, having tripled over

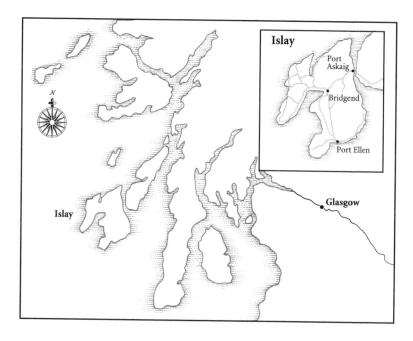

three years, is no longer thought to be in danger of disappearing, and the increase in hunting-permits supplements the island's budget.

In a damp, good-natured crush, everyone ends up finding a place on the packed ferry. The sea is very rough. I watch the men who watch the foam on their beer change course in their glasses as the boat rolls. Whether they are stock-breeders or birdwatchers, they have the same build, like rugby players who have spent their youth battling force fourteen gales: short, strong legs, long torsos, hands like bats and wrists like logs.

The ferry empties out at Port Ellen with a great rattling of chains. Despite my tiredness, I am happy not to have booked accommodation at Port Ellen: such hotels and B&Bs as I can see at a glance are about as appealing as lodgings in a novel by Dickens. I take my bearings: to the east, it's twenty-seven kilometres to the Scottish coast; to the south, Ireland is twenty-three kilometres away; northwards is the romantic island of Mull, at forty kilometres; to the west, the nearest bus-stop is on the coast of Labrador, three thousand eight hundred kilometres away.

104

As the wind blows mainly from the west here, the gusts and waves have time and room to gather speed. The tides are the strongest on the Atlantic coast and transform the straits between the islands into roaring rivers. All of these conditions combine to make the sea around Islay one of the most dangerous in Europe. The island is encircled, as with a baleful necklace, with an infinite number of wrecks, from that of the troop-ship *Tuscania*, torpedoed by a German submarine in 1918 off the Mull of Oa (a hundred and sixty-six lost and a stone memorial in execrable taste), to fishing boats and those of careless amateur sailors. Of these, two hundred and fifty have been identified but there are many unknown others 'lost at sea', like the fishermen in Iceland's waters.* Thus the lifeboat crew in their ultrafast patrol boat, who confront the worst weather and put out over a hundred times a year, are the main beneficiaries of local sponsorship: there isn't a Celtic festival or a fund-raising event where people fail to shell out for a luminous buoy, diving equipment or resuscitation gear.

Ink-black night. From Port Ellen to Bridgend the road is narrow and slippery, as flat as a plank but punctuated by little humpbacked bridges which ford invisible streams level with the peat bog and suddenly lift the car up as though with a malevolent hand. On the slope which descends to the tiny cove of Port Askaig, the headlights catch splashes of colour through the rain: oleanders, bougainvillaea, begonias – vegetation that is almost colonial although at nearly the same latitude as Stockholm. Port Askaig Hotel is a charming, Romantic-period cottage sitting between a kitchen garden and clumps of blood-red dahlias, facing the port. On the façade, neo-Gothic writing tells you that it has been 'Fully licensed since 1835'. It is the oldest inn on the island, where you would not be surprised to find yourself sitting next to the sinister one-legged pirate from *Treasure Island*.

The kilted fishermen from the cove who come here to drink pick up their tammies and *sgian dhus* before they slip into their oilskins to go fishing at dawn. The waitress wears a seaweed-green miniskirt, showing her coltish legs, and has coloured her eyelids the same sea-

---

* French schoolchildren, and no doubt Swiss ones, were familiar with Pierre Loti's classic tale of the Breton fishermen who sailed each summer to the cod-fishing grounds of Iceland, *Pêcheur d'Islande* (1886). Bouvier's grandfather, Pierre Maurice, composed an orchestral suite *Pêcheur d'Islande, Impressions Musicales d'après Pierre Loti* (1895). (Trs.)

green. This red-headed Ophelia is a newcomer, and the old hands don't know how to deal with her. They ply her with arch compliments, to which she remains deaf. The next day, leafing through the local paper, the *Illeach* – published twice a month, half in English, half in Gaelic – I notice that this heartless siren is the subject of a reader's letter. Mr Dave Harris, barman by trade, is upbraiding Mrs Sears, manager of the Port Askaig fully licensed bar, for having chosen this young woman on account of her bosom, build and bottom to attract a 'certain kind of customer'; in short, a very shapely novice who couldn't tell an Alexandra from a daiquiri.

Mrs Sears, whose hair always seems freshly permed, is a woman in her fifties with hard, restless eyes. With her employees and customers she has a Scottish accent, with us an Oxford one. In fact she is English, settled here for thirty years. Besides the fact that they own half the land on the island, many English people occupy influential positions without objections being raised. Of course the Scots were at daggers drawn with their southern neighbours for a thousand years, and despised England. Not all of them, not always, not everywhere: shared legitimate interests often tempered ancestral grudges. Especially here, where there was no room for such resentment: from the twelfth to the end of the fifteenth century the Hebrides, of which Islay was then the capital, constituted an independent maritime empire which often played the English card against the covetous Scottish court. It was not until 1493 that James IV got round to attaching this rebellious archipelago to his kingdom. Thus one finds many English people perfectly at home here. Mostly widows, who sit on the management committee for the ferry service and choose the crêpe-paper to transform little girls into trolls or fairies at the parish fête, by means of a large wrinkled flower pinned to their non-existent bosoms or their rabbit-bottoms.

Mrs Sears's hotel contained what little has been written about the Hebrides, bound in faded pink or green cloth. The first human settlements discovered on Islay date back to 7,000 BC. Hunting, gathering, arrowheads made of flint which was brought from Ireland without getting one's feet wet because, according to glaciologists and prehistorians, the islands were still all joined. Six thousand years later it had changed for good, and for obscure reasons (climate change, forest fires) half the island was covered in a thick layer of peat – fortunately for today's archaeologists because it is a better preservative than ice, and for the distillers who 'smoke' their whisky over peat. The arrival of the Celts (c. 600 BC), the Saxons after the fall of the Roman Empire, and finally the Vikings towards the ninth century AD have not left any written traces. Here and there a burial place. Yet the cemetery on the island of Iona, forty kilometres north of Islay, shelters the ultimate in Merovingian remains.

In the sixteenth century there was anarchy in Scotland and even more in the Hebrides, which wanted to free itself from the stupid and bloody rule of the clans. Islay even produced an 'historic' battle, at Traigh Ghruinneart in 1598, between Sir James MacDonald and his uncle, Sir Lachlan Mor Maclean. There's not an islander today who doesn't claim at least one ancestor who took part in this skirmish. Moreover in the absence of written records, oral tradition has added to the event everything that might satisfy the Scottish imagination, including a hunchbacked, dwarf crossbowman and a witch from the Isle of Mull whose advice was ignored by the Macleans, bringing them death and disarray. A Welsh topographer who visited Islay in the eighteenth century described it as 'a picture of hopeless misery at the world's end'. He did not know that it was about to be bought by a rich merchant who would change its destiny.

Daniel Campbell of Shawfield and his descendants were enlightened entrepreneurs. They drained the marshes, guaranteed their farmers thirty-year leases, founded the town of Bowmore with its school and hospital, introduced flax-growing and the spinning of woollen cloth that was sold throughout Britain, set up a regular ferry service between Port Ellen (which they also founded) and Scotland; and they taught the islanders to fish, which they had never done, by bringing over master fishermen from Spain and... Formosa. The success of these reforms brought with it massive population growth. So around 1850, when the Campbells sold the island to the Morrison family for four hundred and fifty thousand pounds, it was over-populated.

The island's very long history has left few traces. The Vikings destroyed the forts ('duns') built by their predecessors; Cromwell's Roundheads took sledgehammers to the heads of saints and gargoyles; fragments of inscribed or sculpted stone found by labourers in the nineteenth century were sold for shillings to the antiquarians of Glasgow and London; almost all the graves had been visited and pillaged. And anyway there is the westerly wind, which sweeps the island as though it were a ship's bridge, and discourages standing upright: the few menhirs and Celtic crosses spared by the Norsemen and Vikings all lean towards the east, as if they want to lie down on the cropped grass and go to sleep. But not the Kildalton Cross, which has been set upright one more. It is the most important monument on Islay, sculpted *in situ* around AD 800 by a travelling stone-carver, in the style of the crosses on Iona. This man was not overflowing with optimism: despite weathering, you can still identify Cain murdering Abel with the jawbone of an ass; David killing a lion; and Abraham about to kill Isaac to please his Lord. It belongs to a time when people had to put up with unbearable situations. Today, not only do visitors come and spend their holidays here, but the islanders – and this is new – leave for their own holidays in Wales or Provence.

The 9th of August is the most important day of the year in Islay, well ahead of Christmas or New Year. It's Fèis Île, the big agricultural show with races, games, all sorts of animal competitions, and the highest rate of alcohol consumption of the whole summer. Breeding and the dairy industry are still the main enterprises on the island, ahead of the distilleries. Prominent citizens silently manoeuvre to gain the title of High Commissioner of the Fèis Île at least once in their lives. Come rain or wind, the London and Edinburgh bankers who own half the island travel over on that day, with their wives made-up, hatted and gloved. This morning there's a two-hundred-kilometre hole in the cotton covering over the Atlantic, giving us a splendid sky. The show takes place in a huge field, bordered with centenarian elms, west of the Bridgend crossroads. Red-haired kids issue and collect tickets for parking in the windy open air, where the Rollses and Bentleys sit beside muddy tractors, cattle-trailers and Ford Broncos. It isn't just a fair for the landlords, it's for the whole island: everyone is here in their Sunday best, scrubbed up, freshly shaved, soaped, beaming.

As far as the eye can see there are stalls of roasting meat, delicious oysters as plump as fattened chickens, fortune-tellers, clairvoyants, gypsies, pedlars, and above all the pens – mooing, bleating, neighing – where they are putting finishing touches to the grooming, combing and curling of foals, ponies, rams, yellow-eyed goats, ewes and heifers. This excessive and unaccustomed care throws the animals into a panic: the rams charge, the ponies prance on the spot, the bull calves foam, lower their heads and dig in all four hoofs when they are led before the judges. These judges, all male with a red badge in their buttonholes, are a living testimonial to the knitted tie; amiably rubicund and admirably phlegmatic. Leaning on their long carved sticks they wait for the competitors, run experienced hands over the animals' backs, clack their false teeth and make notes in little notebooks.

In the gaps in the hedge that separates the field from a lovely sunken lane, bagpipers are tucked away, cheeks puffed out, scarlet, practising their pieces. The happy atmosphere is invigorating. There is even a competition for well-trained dogs, announced on a poster: 'Anyone may enter any dog as long as it has a foot at each corner'. At the far end of the field there is a huge tent where people can get drunk at their leisure. We are the only foreigners and our accents give us away: lavish rounds of drinks are poured. We are presented to an old man in a kilt and tweed cap who seems to be the island's mascot. He kisses my wife's hand with a worldly little flourish and speaks three words of welcome in French, to cheers. It is Grandpa Duncan, for forty years a stoker on crumbling cargo ships across all the world's oceans.

Back to Port Askaig. On the table in our hotel room there is a note with precise instructions: 'There are no midges in Port Askaig. If you have brought some with you, try the lotion on sale at the grocer's across the road'. In Canada, they call midges *maringouins*. On the continent of Europe, for the good of our health, they do not exist. They are voracious mosquitoes, so small that you only see them as a kind of cloud, whereas they see you very clearly. They hatch in their thousands on the rotting seaweed left by storms or by the high tides in March; and the tons of insecticide needed to kill them off would destroy the Hebridean ecosystem.

The midges go on the rampage around five o'clock in the evening, especially if it's warm and drizzling. Around five-thirty I see the widows, who had been sipping whisky in the garden and carrying on their racy conversation, suddenly picking up their walking-sticks and trotting into the bar, furiously scratching their scalps, eyebrows and ears, which are these creatures' favourite spots. They collapse, laughing, in front of the barmaid and call for their fourth whisky. As for the magic lotion from the grocer, one of the matrons who has covered herself in it is grumbling, 'They seem to love it!', her ears already swollen like apples. The truth is that Islay has the worst midges on the planet, and no antidote works. Only a few privileged people, by dint of being bitten, have reached a state of total immunity.

From my window, I note with satisfaction that the owner of the inn is not one of the elect. I see her, spade in hand, go down to the kitchen garden dressed like an astronaut. I wait to see her leap over a bed of tomatoes in one stride, weightless. No. She stops, begins to dance on the spot, swats wildly, then retreats to her cottage, slamming the door. The English, not without malice, say that the most energetic Scottish dance, the Highland Fling, is simply the result of midges biting and the way kilts make the knees itch.

In the Hebridean world, the only subject of conversation to which midges give way is whisky. The word is derived from the Gaelic *uisge beatha*, which means 'water of life'. The Islay whiskies nearly all have Gaelic names: Laphroaig, Lagavulin, Bunnahabhain, Caol Ila. They are the most expensive whiskies in Scotland and many Scots also regard them as the best. They are drunk from large glasses, without water or ice, like a hundred-year-old Calvados or a vintage Cognac. If you ask for ice in a bar in Bowmore (population four hundred), they will lynch you. These whiskies have a strong aroma of peat, an earthy or, better, subterranean tang, which evokes the caves where naturalists ring thousands of bats. It's such a pronounced taste that during the prohibition era in America the product was freely available as… medicine.

For myself, I prefer the northern whiskies, without peat, like Glenmorangie. Peat comes into play during the drying process, after the grain has been steeped in water and has germinated. It is then turned regularly, traditionally with large wooden shovels. The peat may be added to the fire over which it is dried in kilns. After fermentation and distillation with the excellent water from Islay's springs, a white spirit is obtained, up to sixty-eight per cent alcohol. As with Japanese saké, the quality of the water accounts for half the quality of the whisky. It is then a matter of keeping the whisky for at least five years in oak barrels to give it colour.

The whole process has twelve stages. It should be said that these distilleries provide austere and magnificent architecture, based on functionality. The one at Bowmore, the oldest distillery on Islay (1779), topped by two Ottoman-style towers which are the drying-room chimneys, is halfway between a Turkish bath and a Cistercian convent. Everything there is fantastically clean.

The distillation of first-class whisky requires a great deal of knowledge but is not expensive on Islay. The labour, the water, the peat and some of the barley are already there. The cost price of a good peat whisky is about four pounds per litre. State taxes increase this price by five or six times. It is the main point of friction: the islanders blench when taxes are mentioned, because they can't stand their 'water of life' being considered a luxury product. And the seven distilleries on the island work at half-capacity so as not to put whiskies that have matured for less than eight years on the market, and to maintain the price. They say that there is a whisky from Islay called Bruichladdich. But my tomcat has sharpened his claws on the 'Whisky Map of Scotland' and the names of several distilleries – some of the best – have disappeared. I doubt I'll get over that.

Xian

The Lausanne tourist agency L'Atelier de Voyage *provided the opportunity for Bouvier to go to China three times (in 1984, 1985 and 1986), accompanying a small group of travellers. It was not the way he preferred to travel, but being, he said, 'deaf, dumb and illiterate' in China, he needed arrangements to be made and a local guide was essential. Xian offered a culture that equalled the depth of Kyoto's, in his experience, and a guide who turned out to be precisely on his wavelength.*

Because of the low-lying fog, our plane – although large – circled a long time before landing.

Xian is part of the classical Chinese heartland that holds fog in greater esteem than blue skies. It amused itself here by taking all kinds of forms. On the aspen-lined road that led towards the town the mist went by in dense, oblong flakes like air-balloons, like sticks of candyfloss. Carrying out its misty business at chest-height, hiding us for a moment, separating us completely from the world outside. You had to stretch out an arm to find out what had become of your companions. It was out of one of these cocoons that Monsieur X, who would be our guide to Xian, emerged like a chick from an egg and walked briskly towards us. In Peking we had been guided by two elegant young ninnies in white fishnet tights, who had tottered along, giggling under their parasols, and knew nothing about anything. Ticking off their contracted tasks, they had produced a panda for us – or rather, the suggestion of a panda, as the animal was taking its siesta and we were left speechless before its excrement, steaming under a scorching sun.

I had said to myself 'once is enough', and examined Monsieur X severely. Small, stocky as a *judoka*, a short, thick fringe over his ageless forehead and pupils dilated by atropine. One of the several meanings of Monsieur X's name in Chinese was 'not having', and it certainly seemed that he didn't have anything other than his jacket of gutta-percha yellow, which he might have found on a building site. Sitting beside me at the front of the bus, he let me know by several laconic remarks that he wasn't very happy about being a guide, that he had hoped to be an historian, that as for accompanying tourists, he would have preferred to do it in English, but in that respect, too, he hadn't been given a choice. He turned around and swept a blasé – but curious – glance over my friends, looked at me, and finished his speech, enunciating each syllable, 'the-cir-cum-stances-of-life'. Then, to escape from the professional routine, from the infuriating questions which were always the same, he made as if to sleep. He had crossed his hands on his knees, and held them tight enough to turn his knuckles white. He was about to encounter – like a Swiss mountain shepherd – the seventh or eighth little flock of the year, to be pastured for several days in a fabulous alpine meadow of culture that the Powers had by turns held in contempt, celebrated, reviled, defiled, and, for the last few years, restored to honour (sometimes magnificently restored) for reasons which, after so many recantations, might appear to him – more than to us – dubious. He was regaining his breath and fortitude. Looking sideways at the man pretending to sleep, I saw this: a nail which had been tapped and tapped but had resisted being driven into the beam. A nail both bitter and strong: a hard, square face eloquent of the way a hammer intended to hit you can be made to bounce off. It suggested to me a victory won all alone in black waters of which I knew nothing. Who had tapped without success on that nail? The Party? The Agency whose orders he carried out? The Cultural Revolution? Big Brother? And why? I was in China for the first time, but in Japan, which I knew a little, a proverb assures us that *Kugi wa deru attareru*, The nail that sticks out will be driven in.

It was not for Monsieur X to believe in proverbs, which are all too often a mixture of petty malice and indulgent opportunism. Judging that he had slept enough, this 'nail who stuck out' explained to me that over the years he had collected with great difficulty a little French library, which the Red Guard had burned – he had rescued only the Larousse, which he had wrapped in oilcloth and buried in his garden. When they had slightly loosened the screws, he had learnt this Larousse off by heart, like those peasants in the Haute-Loire who spend the dead season swotting to expand their memory and can place Kashgar or Ushuaia on a map better than any city teacher.

At the hotel, at the end of the morning, outlining the programme for the days to come over a Chinese beer, the sombre Monsieur X astonished us. Not only did words such as *épissure* (splice), *scabreux* (improper) and *réticence* (reluctance) come to him as if he were intimately acquainted with angels, but he used them with extraordinary intuition about a culture with which he wasn't acquainted. They had nothing to do with studiously composed verses on the 'inevitable trio' presented for the admiration of those passing through Xian (the Stele Forest, the Terracotta Army, the Wild Goose Pagoda), nor with demonstrations intended to show off his obviously exceptional mastery of an immense vocabulary. No. These happy turns of phrase came to Monsieur X just as readily when he was faced with the unexpected sights offered by the surrounding markets, streets and villages. But above all, each phrase was constructed, in a syntax more rigid than that of his maternal language, in order that we could grasp the Chinese way (polyphonic, cosmic) of apprehending a bend of the river under willows, a farmer's wife crossing the road and shouting at a sow that had just broken free of her tether, a stele half worn away in the corner of a rice-field, or a bitter, droll episode from his own tribulations. His commentary always put details in perspective and in a revelatory light. Even if he begrudged this tiring work – rushing strangers through a past-present in which too many things still suggested poverty, carelessness, abuses dating back eight or eight hundred years – Monsieur X acquitted himself marvellously. And if he took the risk of making personal comments, it was because he was too well-read and upright to do a slap-dash job and leave us stuck in the rut of official tourism. I say 'past-present' because Monsieur X did not bother to distinguish everyday China from, well, CHINA. For him it was all one. No sooner did we leave the provincial museum, where he had explained the drift of ideograms (a real detective story), than he was sending those of us whose stubble irritated him to be shaved by a barber in the open air, and leading the others into a cheap and smoky restaurant where, after the owner's momentary alarm, we lapped up our bowls of noodles in an atmosphere of friendly curiosity.

It should be said that Xian, over its thirty centuries of existence, had seen the world pass by. It is made of one of the most tightly woven cultural fabrics on the planet: not a clump of peonies without its poet; not a pavilion that hasn't sheltered its favourite or its 'vixen'; not a bridge that hasn't seen the funeral procession of a 'Minister of the Left' or a 'General of the Northern Frontier', in an era when our Charlemagne was still drawing lines and stammering his alphabet under Alcuin's iron rule.

It must be said that forty-five years of totalitarian virtuousness, of sullen rancour coming from the capital, of Stalinist architecture (so-called), of ideological convulsions, have not succeeded in exhausting this fabulous humus that the inhabitants of Xian, despite their still threadbare existence, manage nonchalantly, without pedantry, although a little bit shaken by the discovery of the fabulous 'buried army' which has attracted the whole world to them – all the while considering their Peking cousins as cultural lightweights. It must also be said that the distressing picture of the conditions for the traveller in China that Simon Leys painted in his *Ombres Chinoises* (1974) has been somewhat improved in the intervening ten years. In the free markets, in the frequent unscheduled stops at villages that we requested or Monsieur X made on his own initiative, we came across obvious signs that life was better: brave flotillas of ducks on the ponds or mill-streams beside the road, newly renovated farmyards and thatched roofs, coloured trinkets; at the entrance to courtyards bordered with service-trees, smiles and gestures of welcome, which were no longer the laboured expressions of a 'people's committee'. Monsieur X commented on these small miracles, which so pleased us, with the care of a scalded cat, knowing well that heaven could take back tomorrow what it had given today. And with an edge of bitterness, since this modest and belated fortune mainly benefited the rural areas and certain urban professions (doctors, teachers… guides) hadn't seen anything come their way and didn't hide their pique. Monsieur X said to us, as we were leaving one such farm, 'It's their turn, they were always the turkeys in all the farces, but all the same…'

Perhaps to dampen our enthusiasm, returning from the 'Western Tombs' – which had been so blanketed in fog that the peasants who had had their stalls there for several months, selling toys and coloured knick-knacks and fake or real coins, had packed up and like us were looking rather dumbfounded at the sight of the large stone figures concealed or revealed by the mist – Monsieur X made a stop at a suburb of Xianyang and we went into a small workshop where they made leather silhouettes for Chinese shadow theatres. A clay floor, two carbide lamps coming to the aid of one bare light-bulb hanging from a cord, so weak that it lit up nothing but itself, an improvised stage made of a sheet strung between two bamboo poles and, leaning against the wall or suspended from strings, a host of paper cut-outs: judges, generals, dancers, mandarins, horses, courtesans, demons, some of them silently swaying when the wind blew in from the street. The place was so charged that I suddenly remembered the modest Magic Theatre which the hero of Hesse's *Steppenwolf* strays into one evening when he is in despair, and begins to live again. Monsieur X addressed a few hoarse words to some disembodied voices immersed in their work behind the screen. A blood-curdling cry rang out and the workshop lights went off. On the left of the sheet, a helmeted rider appeared, corseted in his insect armour. It took him about three minutes to cross the stage, making his horse rear and wheel round, cutting and thrusting to get rid of his opponents – ghouls, nomadic archers, and so on – sometimes blurry, sometimes wincingly precise, a swarm of them falling on him from all sides. It was staggering in its virtuosity and magic: I'm sure that I stopped breathing. The soundtrack: perfectly synchronised blows, spiteful grunts, the neighing of their mounts – all these were evoked. We thus saw General Ban Chao cross and conquer Central Asia for China at the beginning of the Christian era. Behind the scenes, the 'troupe' (two exquisitely polite old men and three snotty-nosed kids as lively as weasels, who were their grandchildren) offered us a glass of colourless spirits. The tribulations of this family of puppeteers must have been equal to those of Ban Chao. The parents had 'disappeared' in Shanghai during the black years. The grandparents had had their modest equipment confiscated and were forbidden to practise their eminently popular art, which had been included in the huge catch-all of 'feudal heritage'. For the past few years they had been able to return to their trade, and their repertory, and to make a few pennies by selling their cut-outs to passers-by. 'Things are going better for them at present,' Monsieur X concluded soberly – his ex-jailbird ways had obviously won everyone's trust.

Returning to Xian at nightfall on a road punctured by potholes, cluttered with carts, we saw this: in front of us there was a tractor pulling a trailer, in which pigs were shivering beneath a rope net; the driver, entirely given over to feeling up the peasant girl sitting beside him, was deaf to the furious beeping of the truck trying to pass him. As soon the road allowed, the truck-driver overtook and then turned his vehicle to block the tractor and leapt on its driver to thrash him. The latter, in order to ward off the blows, had withdrawn a huge paw shiny with come from his conquest. The peasants who had pushed their bike-trailers to the side of the road cackled as they separated these two artistes. There was a complete traffic-jam. 'Filming this?' asked Monsieur X. 'Yes' (but night had almost fallen and I could never recover the pictures of this brawl). Monsieur X gave an approving, muffled cackle: the China of Brueghel seemed to please him as much as it did us.

Monsieur X himself, too, pleased us a great deal. We weighed up our chances of stumbling across this humanist. We didn't think of him as an interpreter of culture so much as an active element of it, lively and original, ingeniously uncovering parts of it for us although, by virtue of his function, he should have been denying us access to them. He didn't eat at our table, though – after several attempts to invite him we stopped embarrassing him on this point of etiquette. It is easy – even fashionable – to make fun of such group travel but, for those who neither read nor speak Chinese, it is still the only way to be sure of getting to see something. To launch yourself alone, a deaf-mute in this vast country, is still a thorny business which often ends in defeat and bitterness. And everything depends on the group. My companions (plasterers or manufacturers) were excellent travellers: curious, hardy, patient or complaining when necessary, eyes and ears open to everything that escaped the wooden language of officialdom. They hadn't come as disgraceful burghers of Calais to be given lessons in ideology, they had paid an arm and a leg to see, learn, understand a bit, to be moved, to laugh. In the evening, once the driver had gone home, Monsieur X felt free enough to come and drink at the bar with us, and be infected by 'petit-bourgeois materialism'. He shared reflections or anecdotes that had come to his mind on the bus as we drove back, like a codicil to the day's lessons.

After the first day he had an attitude of friendly brusqueness towards us, giving the lie to Lu Hsun who maintains that the Chinese 'can only consider foreigners as either beasts or superior beings'. We let him know – each in his own fashion – how much we appreciated his work and his company. Walking back with him to his bike, on which he would make the half-hour trip to his little room, I said to him (*bis repetita placent**) 'We arrived in Xian on a truly lucky day,' and saw his troubled expression resolve – as if swept by a lighthouse beam – into a real smile. Not for the last time and I hope it will remain suspended from his handlebars like the moon which slept, that night, on its back.

> The living have such a fear of death that the dead, annoying while they lived, are – with all due rites – whisked away, rejected, forgotten, abolished almost before they have exhaled their last breath (which is the first breath of ghosts and revenants).
>
> Jacques Dars, Aux portes de l'enfer (1984)
(On the attitude of the West towards death)

On the fourth and last day in Xian, around midday, in the beautiful countryside fleecy beneath swathes of mist, our bus overtook a funeral procession which was following the course of a stream down below the road. There were relatives in white mourning clothes, holding branches of willow; four cymbal or tambourine players, and the black lacquered coffin followed by a huge paper dragon in red and blue handled by half a dozen acolytes, its sides opening or closing like an accordion in order to match the curves of the path. Behind, more distant relatives and some kids in caps.

A colourful spectacle (the grass was very green), gracefully and moderately noisy, no lamentations; indeed suggesting that the dead – thus escorted – was more to be envied than pitied. Monsieur X, flushed with excitement (and they say that the Chinese are impassive), muttered, 'This is new... it's come back... never seen this... my father...' What was new was probably not the little procession, but the huge scaly effigy made of oiled paper and light bamboo which, according to Monsieur X, would cost around three months' wages. When I suggested that we abstain from taking photos out of respect for the mourners, Monsieur X contradicted me: the dragon represented a great sacrifice, a decent (therefore happy) way of conducting the dead into the soil; those who had met the cost were rightly proud of it, and nothing would give them more

---

* 'That which pleases is repeated' – Horace. (Trs.)

pleasure than our astonished gaze and our taking photos. No doubt he was right. However I don't recall that any one of us wished to go and join the little cortège. On the one hand because when travelling one must never say to oneself, 'I've got something here,' and wish to turn every moment to account. On the other hand because we all came from a country where death is hidden, where at the end of your journey you leave the house for a ward and from there for a corner of a passage fitted out behind a screen. Nothing at home is more silent nor so well-oiled as a hearse, nor more suffocating than our pallbearers with their white gloves and faces smooth as butter: a silence and blankness frustrating for those who have already cried half their tears, swallowed half their grief. To make a festival for the dead seemed to come from a more dynamic and confident frame of mind. Seeing this convoy winding through the fields, feet damp with dew, with its subdued uproar, its willow branches which would be planted around the grave to grow into trees, its child-followers flabbergasted by the enormous polychrome monster, I wanted to say as St Paul did to the Corinthians, 'O death, where is thy sting? O grave, where is thy victory?' (1 Corinthians 15:55). I wrote down the verse in my notebook and showed it to Monsieur X. '*Aiguillon?*' He raised his eyebrow. An insect's sting. It was the first and the last time (I have seen him since) that I found his vocabulary wanting.

Xian, 1984 – Geneva, 1989

The Roads to Halla-San
or *The Old Shit-Track Again*

In his conversations with Irène Lichtenstein-Fall, Routes et Déroutes *(1992), Bouvier spoke of his intention in* Journal d'Aran et d'autres lieux *of counterpointing the experience of the quintessentially Atlantic island of Aran, a sort of 'western Finnisterre', with that of a tropical island, Jeju. He was intrigued by the 'void' in the Western approach to the Far East. People quite rightly talk up the cultures of Japan and China, he said, yet Korea – as culturally rich as China and moreover the 'mother of Japan' – is scorned and neglected, because of having been a Japanese colony for forty-five years. Bouvier recalls his Korean journey, made in 1970, as a very happy period in his life: he had been working hard and thus had money to spend on travel; he enjoyed having his wife's company; also, because of their years in Japan, they were able to speak Japanese to Koreans over forty who had been forced to learn it, but didn't mind speaking it to foreigners. He preserved particularly vivid images of these travels, and let them mature over twenty years before he began to write. He wanted to describe Korea without any trace of exoticism, he said, 'as though I were describing a journey around Burgundy, because I had so quickly become familiar with its very distinctive cultural and moral climate'.*

Prelude to Korea
Kyoto, 1970
Right beneath our old house, below the uneven, ghostly stairway up Yoshida-Shimoodji, between a tuft of willow-herb and a rowan tree, there is a Korean rotisserie no bigger than a Normandy sideboard. There isn't room to swing a cat. It's run by a widow and her daughter. When I sit down, the mother comes and sits opposite, sets a brazier on the plank that serves as a bar, and makes me a meal by grilling tiny pieces of red or yellow meat (dog? Horse off-cuts?) marinated in a garlic sauce; they get covered in fine ash and turn the colour of her face. She draws on the fag placed askew in her *kiseru* (a bamboo cigarette-holder, with a little brass end shaped like the bowl of a pipe), and looks at me without saying a word. Her smooth, grey face mingles patience, malice, a wisdom that knows how to hunker down and wait, and pride in being – with her daughter – the only foreigners in business in this neighbourhood.

You have to live here to appreciate the victory this represents. Most Japanese pay scant attention to Korea and the Koreans, forgetting what they owe to the culture that brought them, among other things, Chinese writing, Buddhism, some of the arts of fire, various kinds of divination, and some magical animals. In return for such gifts, the Japanese sent over pirates tattooed from head to foot, devastating military expeditions and, from 1910 to 1945, colonial bullying and blows, after the West had deprived Japan of its slice of the Chinese cake and of its victory against the Russian Empire and had thrown it Korea like a bone to a dog. 'I shall whip you with scorpions,' declared the Japanese Governor-General of Korea, Terauchi, to his citizens in 1916, when the Koreans were trying to attract the Allies' attention to the fate of their country. He did his best to keep his word: three years later, during non-violent demonstrations, eight thousand Korean civilians died, fifteen thousand were injured and fifty-seven thousand were arrested. In 1969, a Japanese historian thus wrote that compared to the Japanese occupation of Korea, that of Czechoslovakia by the Russians was 'just a picnic'. During the thirty-five years of total domination, many Korean peasants dispossessed by absentee landlords went in search of a pittance in Japan, swelling the urban proletariat, thieving on a small and large scale, without ever becoming integrated. They live on the margins here; they are the *Graeculi* (little Greeks), the emancipated slaves of comedies by Terence and Plautus, often smarter than their masters. The Japanese envy them their impertinent resourcefulness, their genius for swindling, and say when they are conned, tapping their foreheads in vexation, '*Kankokujin, atama ga ioi!*' ('The Koreans had me there!'). They have to 'have them' to survive in a society that ignores or rejects them, and page 3 of the papers features the often hilarious swindles and tricks of these Asiatic layabouts.

For all these reasons, the widow readily sits down opposite me and cooks me meat that's tougher than leather. I, too, am a foreigner. Back in Korea, she had a husband, a petrol pump, and a little repair shop at the southern exit from Gwangju, for a thousand years the town of hotheads, rebel poets and students, a nightmare for the central power, whether in Seoul or Tokyo. Everything was blown away by bombs and napalm fire. Now she has this minuscule bar, this beautiful daughter, as hard as iron, who assists her and no doubt lets others share her bed sometimes, and a sturdy grandson of five or six, his shaven head covered in white powder against the prickly heat, who imitates all the television cartoon heroes in a sepulchral voice, respects nothing (how refreshing, here), and whose father is also a shadow. From time to time an exhausted hack, a surgeon from the nearby hospital, or one of the symbolist poets (numerous here, among the peonies and wisteria), wearing a Basque beret in homage to France, comes to collapse like a sparrow fallen from its nest in the corner of the bar. They quickly become tipsy – just a sip of alcohol will do it here – and moan amusingly about married life, touchingly vulnerable and open as though we knew each other well, leaving me their addresses which I later lose. Find me a more pleasant spot! It is in this floating world, a bit woozy on saké, that I make my rare, fleeting, Japanese friendships…

I was the last customer. After I had paid, the daughter gave me a tight little smile, aimed like an arrow to reach me and no farther,

126

and as I crossed the threshold she tugged my shirt-tail, which was not tucked in, to let me know that she was on her own, while her mother observed this ploy serenely like a good madam, knowing what was what, expert at extracting pennies. Outside the night was exquisite, the ground loosened by the light May rain that falls and disappears. She caught up with me in the street to give me the towel and soap that I'd left on the counter – I'd come from the public baths. She walked beside me, in silence. Twenty-five, thirty years old? Really lovely, and supple like a rod of steel. I like women who move without making a sound and whose eyes swim with the purest water. If my heart had not belonged elsewhere, I might have followed her. All the same, the red meat she sliced up all day long and her blue steel knife would doubtless have given me pause. And to have attained this degree of silence, she might be a vixen. Foxes are the servants of the spirit Inari, patron of rice-growing and profitable negotiations. Vixens, on the other hand, are formidable magicians who, in the form of dizzyingly elegant seducers, can lead a man, a clan, an empire to their ruin before going back to their red fur and the silent night of the woods. From their ancient home in India, country of reincarnation, these cunning tricksters crossed Tibet and reached China where, transformed into pernicious favourites who offered bad advice, they had pushed the last emperors of the Jin dynasty into such iniquitous behaviour that they lost the throne. In the eighth century AD, the Japanese envoy Kibi No Makibi, returning from a cultural mission the main object of which was to steal the lunar calendar from the Chinese, left the west coast of Korea without realising that one of these witches – *kitsune* in Japanese – had boarded his junk. Her arrival on the archipelago in 758 was soon followed by political unrest, palace revolution, and an attempt to unseat the bonze Do-kyo. Reckoning that she had caused enough mayhem, the vixen disappeared for two centuries, busying herself giving numerous progeny to the world. In the tenth century, the astronomer Abe No Yasuna, a fervent Buddhist, saved a wounded fox from a hunt, and found her to be a *kitsune*. As a token of her gratitude, she took the form of the fiancée for whom Yasuna was waiting, gave him three years of happiness and a son and, having paid her debt, disappeared, leaving this poem on a paper window-pane:

So It Goes

> *Koishiku ba*
> *tazunekite miyo*
> *izumi naro*
> *shinoda no more no*
> *urami kuzunoha*

> If you still love me
> in the depths of the wood of Shinoda
> where the spring rises
> you will find as a souvenir
> a leaf of arrowroot

As you would expect, Abe No Seimei, the son of the astronomer and the vixen, was a formidable magician, and is often shown in drawings as cutting through the night on a bat's back. He was able to identify *kitsune* and unmasked one who, in the form of a Japanese empress, caused consternation throughout the country by her extravagance. Even to this day, in the Fukui Prefecture opposite Korea, certain well-off peasant families are said secretly to raise vixen, and are more feared than the plague.

I had to read this poem to realise that a few vixen had already passed through my insignificant life. Obviously without my knowing. So I stick to the rules.

The 'old shit-track'
Kyoto, 1970
'Enter the body, leave the body, and find your freedom' – thus Chan Buddhism of the T'ang dynasty and Japanese Zen Buddhism. All creation, I would even say all existence worthy of the name, goes through these three essential stages and, for me, inner freedom is certainly the only thing worth risking your skin for in this world of illusion. Such an undertaking, always dangerous, assumes many forms, and writers such as Kafka, Katherine Mansfield and Henry Miller (among many others) have not relied on Buddhism in throwing themselves wholeheartedly into it, or have achieved Zen without knowing it, like M. Jourdain speaking prose.˙ The assiduous asceticism

of Japanese monasteries, like the stern Rule of the Carthusians or the Trappists, is not for everyone. Not having practised either of these, I proceed cautiously here, but I have been close enough to them to know cases in which the cure has been worse than the disease, where I have seen characters, even strong ones, destroyed by the aridity and requirements of these disciplines. Bitter, defrocked monks, apprentice Buddhists trapped 'in the flesh' as in the barrel of a gun, unwilling to throw in the sponge, not daring to take a step forward or retrace their steps. Even if Zen Buddhism is, if you believe R. H. Blyth (who knows what he's talking about), 'Asia's greatest treasure', there are other ways to gain knowledge and liberty. Eroticism for Tantric philosophy, opium for Thomas De Quincey, absinthe for Verlaine, walking for Rimbaud, the sea for Conrad: everyone finds his own key. And no heavenly law obliges us to choose the most stubborn.

For our friend Dick, it is Korea. When he can no longer bear the ceremony of the monastery where he has worn himself out in meditation for four years, when the koans (the riddles or paradoxes set for novices) leave him tongue-tied, when the bullying of his *roshi* (master) – an everyday experience for Zen apprentices – makes his ears swell up and when the nasal tone of the Japanese scholars he mixes with gets on his nerves, he goes off to Korea for a supply of insolence, impulsiveness and freshness. A fine therapy to which he has resorted several times. He folded up a route map covered with annotations, exclamation marks, circles in various coloured inks, and offered it to me, laughing, with the words: 'Keep an eye on your bag, hide your dough, and watch your step. It's not Japan any more, it's the old shit-track again.' We shall see.

This year the Japanese press has begun to refer obliquely to the 'Korean miracle', but the per capita income in Korea is still no more than a sixth of that in Japan.

The huge scar which criss-crosses Dick's semi-shaven skull, as though from trepanning, comes from another Korea, experienced

---

* Monsieur Jourdain, who wants to rise above the middle class in Molière's *Le Bourgeois Gentilhomme* (1670), thinks he has a difficult task ahead of him in learning to speak 'prose', but is delighted to discover that he has been speaking it for the past forty years without realising it. (Trs.)

in uniform. At least I suppose so, I don't know; he never talks about it. And despite the friendship that is developing, cautiously, between us, I wouldn't ask him: there are things that simply aren't worth revisiting. In a work about the fighting in Seoul in 1950, I came across a report by Rutherford Poats, then a foreign correspondent for United Press. A little girl burnt by a phosphorus shell walked up to a roadblock held by marines.

> She was blinded and one wondered how she could still be alive. She was about the same height as my daughter. Three other Korean children who had been luckier than her watched her approach and stumble over the pavement. She had to pick herself up three times before she clambered on to it. The children were laughing.

A little piece of theatre among thousands of others that, for me, reveals an absolute evil. Someone who has lived through that, as an actor or a powerless observer, can no longer be content to live without trying to understand it. So they look for the answer in drugs, alcohol or – what is much more worthwhile, even if it is a false trail – in mental asceticism and meditation.

On the boat between Kobe and Fukuoka, Japan
June 1970
Women who have led 'a life of pleasure' and retained their health have – like those spinning-tops children whip along – built up a speed at which they absolutely must operate. When they age, they make themselves useful in a hundred ways. This one is slight and mercurial, her silvered hair clipped back with two tortoiseshell combs in the shape of doves, wearing Chinese-style black trousers and minuscule felt slippers on her baby feet. The group of gossips around her don't absorb all her energy or her interpersonal skills. She's bored, and her eyes rest on us for a moment – we are the only foreigners on the ferry – on the lookout for the slightest excuse to approach us. I had taken photos of her while she was massaging some old ladies of the same type who had backache, handling them as though trussing chickens, foraging under their

skirts amidst dirty laughter. We encountered her again the next day at dawn, in the canteen, in the queue for the morning soup of red beans. She smiled, revealing perfect teeth, and opened her purse under my nose to show me that it was almost empty. An excellent introduction. Then she put her expert hand on Eliane's stomach to see whether anything was moving round inside it. To avoid unnecessary advice, I told her that we already had children. While she was asking our ages, she was already busy with her fingers, hard as ebony, kneading my wife's neck, which she perceived to be a bit stiff. The sun rises, red as an apple, over a sea of snub-nosed, good-natured faces, split by huge yawns. She is 81 (one confidence deserves another) and tells me that in the old days she was so pretty that men gathered round her like wasps on a jam sandwich. She had never been ill and always looked after others. Once she had broken a leg kicking the private parts of a gentleman who was not to her liking. She obviously didn't count the abortions or gonorrhoea which, for her, were the accidental consequences of work.

'Are you from Kyushu, grandmother?' (I had often come across such cheerful old hussies in Kyushu.)

'*Daïtaï Tokyo des*' (from near Tokyo).

It was the same as saying 'near Paris', as a countrywoman from Yvelines would say to impress a stranger, or 'from around Tokyo' in the days of the Japanese Mikado brothels, where she grew up fast and got her diploma. I have a lot of respect for these old, rebellious madams, so well groomed, who settle the problem of *communication* – much discussed here – by putting a hand on a stomach or a thigh, by carrying off screaming babies who calm down at once, to the embarrassment of their mystified mothers, while using a free hand to warm fresh eggs for a one-eyed companion who is weighed down by varicose veins, and who slowly gulps the eggs through a hole she has pierced with her hairpin. In her *obi* (kimono belt) she has another wallet, full to bursting. The empty one she shows is just for laughs.

The first-class passengers have a Japanese bath and the company provides them with fine blue-and-white-striped dressing-gowns. In fact on this ferry everything is very clean and well laid-out, but it's obviously on our level, in steerage, that everything happens, where the best Go players congregate, the best insults are exchanged, where you can hear the lovely fishers' songs from the west coast, where Rabelasian friendliness is at its best. Emboldened by a few beers, the well-to-do from the upper deck come down to join in our games with the groggy, beseeching air of those who have paid a high price for the slender privilege of being left alone.

Fukuoka-Hakata, Japan
June 1970

The New City hotel between Fukuoka and the port had been built so quickly to accommodate the overflow from the World Fair in Osaka, or foreigners in transit to Korea, that they had forgotten to advertise its existence. It doesn't feature in any guide, there's no sign pointing to it, and we stumbled on it by pure chance, just as the last painter in the building was cleaning his last brush. The receptionist knows five hundred words of English; the cashier, fifty; the lowest kitchen-boy about a dozen. The flowers in the room were fresh this morning but the hotel, open for a week now, is absolutely empty, and half the staff – a very bad sign – have already bitten their nails to the quick. Each time we step over the threshold, three boys of sombre distinction in frogged frock-coats, a trifle gay, rush to relieve us of even the humblest parcel.

The Westerners visiting Japan this year were not going to Korea. If they knew the name Seoul, it was because of a hot war which had narrowly avoided triggering a third world war. If they went into raptures – with good reason – over Chinese or Japanese civilisation, they knew nothing at all, or hardly anything, of the magnificent Korean culture. As for the Japanese, a survey I'd read recently claimed that, of all the countries in the world, Korea was the one they found least attractive: a colony they'd lost, where they'd been unwelcome, where all the meals smelled of garlic… Thus the hotel is empty. On the table, a message signed by one Yuji Sonobe, manager, urges us to relax in the '*Champignon*' Bar and to try the specialities of the '*Blue Grata*' restaurant on the first floor. The restaurant being empty, the cook has turned off his ovens, and if you are hard-hearted enough to want to eat all the same, he shamelessly goes in search of a meal for you from the Corona Hotel, the competitor across the road.

Moving from one culture to another, words like these go adrift in strange ways. In the West, oriental vocabulary (from India, China or Japan) immediately gives off a whiff of incense or opium and acquires an aura of esotericism. The Orient has to be portrayed as esoteric; any word, even the most concrete, will do the trick. Conversely, from the early 1970s the Japanese, who mainly knew the world through what they read, were beginning to discover that the aura of glamour through which they refracted their understanding meant that they sometimes lost sight of the actual meaning of foreign words. Thus, since the French were credited with inventing *amour*, everything expressed in French had the scent of forbidden fruit. I remember a bar in Kawaramachi (Kyoto), its erotic-surrealist atmosphere based on Georges Bataille or Joyce Mansour, where the students in fishnet stockings crossed their legs revealingly, and when they looked at you, always ran a little pink tongue-tip lasciviously across their lips. This bar – I hope it hasn't changed its name and that you can find it – was called *Ambiance famille* (Family Atmosphere)…

This empty hotel! I wonder what reading or games while away the time for the richly brocaded employees. If I were Phileas Fogg or Barnabooth, I would put a leather holdall stuffed with banknotes on the counter, and send them all off on holiday. This white, empty hotel is like a bride whose groom has been struck by lightning on the church steps. Those deals and loans made at optimistic, unsteady dinners… now: this waiting. A baby cockroach hauls itself up, with difficulty, on the rim of the brand new enamel washbasin. There is nothing for him to do here, bad errand-boy from the depths of the drains. He is as red as a freshly varnished violin; his antennae tremble and say, 'Monsieur Sonobe: bankrupt.' He has come to repossess the place, ahead of the bailiffs.

Busan, Korea
June 1970
Apart from the fifty-six thousand GIs cooped up in their houses and barracks, there are few foreigners here. So the Koreans look down their noses at travellers, somewhat alarmed. They come as close as a dentist, then, their curiosity satisfied, they move off, sometimes

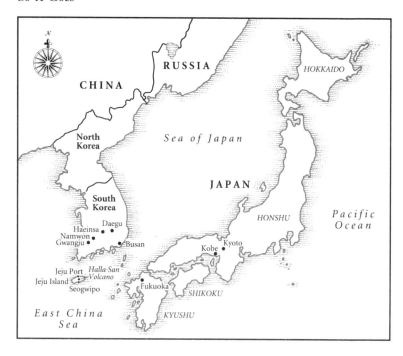

with a quick nod, or a snicker. You have to get used to it, but it wasn't always like this. At the beginning of the twentieth century Korean society was suffocated by smug Confucianism, starchy, mannered formality, grumpy misogyny and xenophobic chauvinism; calcified and excluded from history, to the point of being easy prey for all kinds of hunger. The reformist patriots emerging from the 'enlightened' Japanese universities of the Meji era let air into this sealed room. Christian missionaries – Catholic or Protestant – often persecuted and never well in with those who counted, brought the rudiments of hygiene to the countryside, and education to girls and hope to believers, unhesitatingly paying a price – years in prison, the executioner's block or gallows. Along with the 'reductions', settlements created by the Jesuits in Paraguay in the eighteenth century, this was an example of a liberating evangelism, to which even an unbeliever takes off his hat: a decent, moral liberation, on top of which there is the cynical and savage insolence of people that have twice passed through a storm of iron and fire, have lost everything, have seen seventy per cent of their country reduced to ashes. The miracle is that the survivors of this apocalypse should have kept so busy for seventeen years in an ocean of rubble, maintaining an appetite for life and battling on, ready to patch up everything with whatever comes to hand, as fast as possible.

Busan II

'The old shit-track'? And how! As soon as you arrive, it's immediately apparent that everything is more modest, patched, basic than in Japan, new buildings starting to crumble before they're completed. Even the grass seems to have been bungled by some unemployed botanist, bristling and grey with cement dust. The dung-flies fly too low for the swallows and do very well thank you. Even if Busan had never been bombed or shelled by the Communists, the almost total destruction of the country is still visible everywhere. At customs, a fellow in straw sandals and prison-style garb sprayed us with insecticide like cattle– 'Close your eyes, please' – using a hose and a vaporiser with straps, straight out of the scrapyard. Another screened our backpacks with a rusty metal detector from the MacArthur era, on which – if you peered – you could see the word *fuck* written years ago by a disheartened GI, a palimpsest washed over by seventeen monsoons.

The Korean is quick-tempered. Unless very wise or very old, he is excessively curt with everyone. As soon as the plane doors open, there is a frantic stampede towards customs and immigration by countrymen laden with presents bought in Japan. Frantic and futile: the officers won't hurry up for so little. Several demi-johns of saké are broken in the crush and we stand for an hour under a blazing sun amidst the powerful smell of rice wine.

'Change? Change dollars?'

Someone grabs me by the elbow and trots me along to a freshly plastered hut, where a 'Bank' sign is hanging. As the concrete has cracked while drying, the door sticks; we crawl on all fours under the counter to reach the 'banker', to whom I have to suggest a yen exchange rate. Happily, he takes my word for it. Right opposite there is another counter: 'Tourist Information'.

'We would like to get to the Haeinsa Temple this evening – when is the next train for Daegu?'

'You have to ask at the station,' reply two Korean girls, wearing the beautiful white national dress *à la Récamier* and gracefully fanning themselves.

'And the express bus?'

'We don't know anything about timetables – just a few words of English,' they add, giggling, putting their hands over their mouths. 'Bon voyage in Korea.'

Intrigued by our backpacks, two drunks approach, raising a cloud of dust, assuring us of their goodwill. They are absolutely smashed and without the coolie-style headbands round their foreheads, they would explode. Their faces are brick-red, their cheekbones almost luminous, a sign to Koreans to wisely change direction to avoid them. They go off, arguing noisily.

We climb into a compartment of the Busan-Seoul express (all in purple velvet), which has just begun operating. Viennese waltzes over the loudspeaker, the carriage almost empty. Some officers in impeccably ironed tunics, caps on their knees, sleep open-mouthed as we roll along the broad, magnificent valley of the Nakdong River.

Towards Daegu

The light is retreating and taking the colours with it, one by one: the flat grey of the river, the fading green of its banks, the mauve of the mountains – haunches, groins, shoulders – formed like half-buried women. Tiny junks on the river, out of scale, with their sails carefully patched and their nets on poles. On the banks, boys blackened by sun skimming stones at nightfall. In the sky, white-tailed sparrow hawks circling. This 'express' stops – all the better – at every little station.

Seen from the train, a hundred details suggest that we're back on terra firma, that without the boundaries and bullshit of politics, a man in good health and working order could, in a little over two years, get back to Geneva, the Loire or Brittany on foot, without dawdling but no great effort either. What evokes this continental continuity, in a landscape as Asiatic as a lecturer or missionary with an epidiascope could wish, is – for example – a patch of dahlias under a service tree in a small courtyard of brown earth; washing hanging above a big tomcat, fast asleep, while a goose circles and contemplates pecking him; a magpie dropping a marrowbone, which is immediately covered in a swarm of ants – in short, those little things in which one can take pleasure without moving far from home, the micro-spaces whose composition no longer reminds one of Hokusai, but instead of Benjamin Rabier.* While there are magpies in Japan, too, they are *sumi-e* magpies ('black-ink painting', with ink and brush), exempt from reality and our envy because of the admirable Japanese talent for abstraction. There's no question of putting them in the stockpot, as any decent family of Savoyard basket-makers would do. Here, on the border of Asia and Europe, such abstraction no longer exists.

Eurasia certainly exists. Herodotus, born near Bodrum in Asia Minor, had good reason for wanting to reconcile the Persians with the Greeks in his *Histories*. Alexander the Great was right in pushing his Macedonian captains into marriage with the daughters of the Achaemenid aristocracy. On the banks of the Yamuna – a tributary of the Indus – his successor, Menander (second century BC), argued over the nature of the vital principle, the atomic weight of the soul and the notion of illusion with the Buddhists of Ashoka's empire. Perhaps it was necessary for the Greek rhetoricians to travel that far to find their equals in splitting hairs. Much later still, Ögodai Khan's Mongols on their little horses were not disconcerted to find themselves carried to the gates of Trieste, and continued to desecrate, destroy and burn – when they could – the attributes of settled life – trees, books, houses – as they had done the whole length of their mighty journey. Nothing suggests that the emissaries of the Pope and St Louis to the court of the Mongol khans were wide-eyed with dismay at the spectacle of Karakoram, the huge, temporary capital of felt tents, where they were given a friendly welcome, and were the objects of curiosity. Whereas nine centuries earlier the Roman historian Ammianus Marcellinus had portrayed such nomads as coming straight out of the devil's cauldron, the emissaries were keen to claim them as descendants of one of the twelve tribes, and were full of praise for their code of law, *yasser*, which severely punished adultery, theft and breaking one's word. The emissaries' understanding was the fruit of the leisurely way they travelled, on mules, yaks or camels. Such continuity also finds

---

* Rabier (1864–1939), French illustrator, animator and comic-book artist, who created – among other things – '*la vache qui rit*'. (Trs.)

expression in Marco Polo's *Devisement du monde* – his 'travels' – written a little later, in which I find no hiatus: the admiration he feels does not indicate that he is out of his depth or raving. If, here and there, a dragon breathes out smoke or a unicorn passes between two copses, it is because these are already part of the Eurasian imagination, and have been for a long time. Anyway, the Venetian readers didn't attach any importance to these allegorical trifles and read his book like good grocers, just as people read the *Wall Street Journal* today: for the price of lapis lazuli, transit times, sheltered anchorage; for solid stuff, 'commerce and trading' (*de la mercadence et de la trafique*), as Montaigne later described the conquest of the New World.

It's easy to swim across the Bosphorus. The passes over the Khyber or the Khunjerab (which gives access to Chinese Turkestan) can be crossed in winter as well as summer. This continuity exists. I experienced it – as a temporary hand on a dig in Bactria – on coming up with a handful of earthy coins from the first century BC, which bore inscriptions front and back in Greek, Indic and Chinese. And rediscovered it, forty years later, in Turpan, in Xinjiang, listening to the wonderful music of the Uighurs, their red-blooded, rough voices, their almost gypsy strain. After some years of living in Japan, it was inexplicably reassuring to detect the continuity here.

Daegu, the same evening

The station, an unfinished mass of concrete, is a long way from the centre. A strong evening wind blows dust over the silhouettes of travellers bent over their luggage. It's an interminable conglomeration – I couldn't possibly call it a town – wounded, blackened, crapulous, in which new buildings already look like ruins. Along with Oshamambe (north Japan) and Rădăuți (in Ceaucescu's Moldavia), it wins the prize for the place to leave as soon as possible, for fear of incalculable consequences. But there we were, there was nothing going farther southwest and so we had to stay the night. As it headed for the centre, the bus bounced over potholes. Each time the driver honked the horn, a plastic mandarin orange hanging from the rear-view mirror lit up and sparkled pathetically. The economic miracle!

We struggled to find a *yogwan*, a traditional, reasonably priced guesthouse. Ours was barely finished: the smell of shit fought with that of newly mixed cement. On the other side of the muddy street, pockmarked with puddles draining away the end of the day, there were cops, an ambulance, stretchers in front of what was perhaps a bakery, its metal shutters half-closed. The owner, who spoke good Japanese, welcomed us graciously. She explained the police presence to us: in the morning, a plainclothes inspector who was investigating suspicious trade wanted to use the telephone in the shop. When he could not get a connection, he smashed the receiver against the wall. The baker and his furious brother smashed his skull. The call was traced, other cops descended and, finding their colleague in a bad way, beat his murderers to death. The three bodies had just been picked up. No time wasted: exactly that quick temper I mentioned earlier.

An absolutely bare room. Two thin mattresses placed side by side on the chocolate-brown linoleum, two pillows the size of cherry-stones. An inn for small-time hookers: next to the mattresses, the wall is starred with chewing-gum, stuck every which way by the girls when their clients required their mouths. No stopping here longer than was necessary.

Daegu bus station

An economic take-off against a background of shortages, shards and rubble has to go through a stage of 'temporary improvement' which, in an urban setting, can only be appalling: jerry-building with whatever can be salvaged from the ruins, re-using any old thing and patching it up. This urban shoddiness disappeared when we reached the countryside, just as poor, but where the simplicity of the traditional materials – tiles, thatch, rush screens, unfired brick – prevented this stage from being squalid.

Four years ago the poet and traveller Lorenzo Pestelli constructed the word *armisère* for South Korea, out of *armée* and *misère*, figuring that only the army and the cops, guarantors and beneficiaries of an authoritarian police state, had enough to eat.

Life has changed since then. Despite the corruption of officials who extract their usual toll, the hundreds of millions of dollars (as war reparations or low-interest loans) injected into the Korean economy by Japan eventually trickle down and guarantee a slender viaticum for even the poorest. The curtness, the lively gestures, the impatient glances found everywhere also say, 'The worst is behind us, we're recovering.' On the other hand, the crimes and abuses of the North Koreans when they occupied the country as far as the outskirts of Busan have left behind such fear, such enduring hatred, and the Pyongyang regime is so loathed by the underground left, that even the students opposed to those in power undertake their two years' national service without too much grumbling.

Bus from Daegu to Deokam-ri, the same day
The bus-conductors here are lasses of fifteen or sixteen, sturdy and squat, their hair divided into two thick plaits, sticky with dust from the road; they appear to have no fear of God or the Devil. Having grown up in a world that lacked everything, and learned to survive in it, they are harder than bricks. They keep a sharp eye on passengers and are quick to do battle with the 'bad 'uns' – drunks, tattooed ruffians and pickpockets. No one bothers to help them in their disputes with these hooligans; they let loose a volley of shrill abuse, hit them, and try to collar them and throw them off the bus. When these actions do not work, they kneel by the driver, bursting into hysterical tears. The driver, who already has enough to do with the bumpy road and the juddering steering-wheel dislocating his shoulders, then stops the bus and gets up to eject the trouble-maker with one blow. This time they'd both had to use strong-arm tactics on a vindictive drunk who, moreover, hadn't paid his fare. There he is on the side of the road, dazed by the slapping. The lass gets down again to bawl him out and kick his sides. When I asked her to tell us the stop for Deokam-ri, she looked at me with the unblinking stare of one who doesn't understand a word. On arrival, though, she pulls us out of our seats and hurls our packs on to a little square where the wind is whipping up the dust. At one end, a cop is dozing on a chair outside his sentry-box; at the other, a woman squats in her immaculate white dress, talking furiously through tears while peeling hard-boiled eggs. Up in a service tree, a loudspeaker – still connected, the devil knows why – is broadcasting the theme tune

of *Un homme et une femme* across this back of beyond. In the rice-fields down below the square, women in coloured aprons have begun planting. They are advancing slowly in a line, up to their knees in water, to the sound of a little drum beaten in three-four time by a lad sitting beside the low enclosing wall. We set out on foot towards the temple. A humid heat, early afternoon. Flocks of loud hawks under a white sky.

Haeinsa I

When the 'good law' of Buddhism reached the west coast of Korea at the end of the fourth century AD, it was faced with a traditional shamanic culture (still in existence) which had already encountered Taoism and Confucianism. Buddhism adapted well to Taoist or 'magic' practices, as it had in China. When things heated up, those in power begged bonzes and *mudang* (priestesses) to mount the barricades together, with their spells and mantras. As for Confucianism, from the Koryo dynasty (907–1390) onwards – and as in China – the relationship was a continual trial of strength. At the time this temple was built in the late eighth–early ninth century, Korea, unified under the Silla dynasty (52 BC–AD 907), had been liberated from the control of the Tang, to whom they paid symbolic tribute of finely wrought gold, horses and tiger-skins, and with whom they maintained very good relations. The Koreans at this time were incomparable goldsmiths and the best bell-founders in the whole of the Far East. Built in places carefully and marvellously chosen by geomancy, large monasteries ruled over vast estates of forests, rice-fields, vegetable gardens, mulberry trees and silkworms, and played the same spiritual and cultural role as the medieval abbeys in Europe. Many Korean bonzes and scholars went to study in China; some of them even made the long voyage to India, in the footsteps of Faxian and Xuanzang. Many of these monasteries, where monks and nuns lived side by side, were built either on a mountain or a mountainside, which – as Taoists believed – encouraged the exchange of earthly and heavenly energies, Yin and Yang.

After the year 1000, the power of these monasteries grew because they were expected to work miracles when there was any threat in the offing. Most often this was to do with making rain with the aid of shamanist soothsayers in times of drought, and they seem to have succeeded often enough for their immense privileges to be confirmed with gifts of land and exemptions from taxes and labour. Such prosperity and impunity leads to decline: a priesthood on the one hand specialising in spells and 'abracadabra', on the other, becoming secular and bloated. The bonzes fattened up and became debauched at the expense of their serfs; the splendid sacred art of the Silla era became trivial, leaden, over-stuffed. By a just reversal, the very thing that caused Buddhism to be a worldly success led to its downfall. In 1231, the Mongols crossed the Yalu River and sacked the North Kingdom. The royal court, holed up on the fortified Gangwha Island on the Han River, secured their retreat with a heavy tribute of gold and especially those furs which the barbarians used for their hats. (Before he unified the rival clans and was named the 'Great Khan', Genghis – who had died three years previously – was hunting on skis for otter and mink in the Orkhon forests to feed his family, after a plot had sent them into exile.) Conscious of standing alone in the face of the greatest military power of the time, the Koreans put this brief respite to good use by engraving the entire canon of Indian Buddhist scriptures on hardwood blocks, thus attracting Heaven's protection. As Korean script would not be invented for another two centuries, the transcription was in Chinese characters. The endeavour began in 1236 and was completed about fifteen years later. More than eighty-one thousand blocks were engraved, ready for printing. This devotional act – also a magical undertaking – had no effect. Two years after the completion of the great work, Möngke Khan returned with his squadrons and seized the whole kingdom, which remained under the domination of the Sino-Mongol Yuan dynasty for over a century.

At this defeat, which discredited the occult powers of Buddhism, the Confucians rejoiced and crowed. One of them, at the end of the fourteenth century, wrote to the king: 'A state which is on the road to prosperity listens to the people;... a state which is going to wrack and ruin listens to deities; serving Buddha and the deities does not bring any advantage.' A return to the moralist's wagging finger and stay-at-home pragmatism.

It is a real miracle that this enormous labour, known today as the 'Korean Buddhist Canon' – Tripitaka Koreana – escaped woodworm, fire, the Mongols, the Japanese condottiere Hideyoshi's invasion attempts (in 1590 and 1598), and above all the storm of steel and fire, the pitiable and bloody ebb and flow of the Korean War. This colossal compendium of engraved blocks was moved circa 1398 to the monastery towards which we are climbing, as large drops of warm rain begin to speckle the dusty road. The blocks remain to this day, and make Haeinsa the greatest 'wooden library' in the world.

Haeinsa II

The bed of the mountain-stream which runs down Mt Kaya and soaks the terraces west of the monastery is a book in stone. For eleven centuries pilgrims have etched thousands of votive inscriptions in Chinese characters and, from the fifteenth century, in the magnificent Korean syllabary on the riverside rocks and on the stones that emerge in the dry season. Many are so profound and so expertly inscribed that one imagines they took at least a week to write. Pilgrims are rarely in a hurry, and to sculpt such large rocks is such an absorbing task that they could get caught up in it and not notice the days going by. Centuries of floods and monsoons have washed and polished these prayers or thanksgivings, have given them a patina and smoothness so 'natural' that the human hand is forgotten, as if these prayers were born from the stone itself, which spoke in our favour.

For the fifteen kilometres that the path runs alongside the stream you won't find a surface larger than two-hands' breadth that hasn't been put to use. As I walked up this immense prayer book of rock between the thorn bushes, I cursed my ignorance: I cannot read either Chinese ideograms or the Korean alphabet. It would take several Faustian lifetimes laboriously to decipher the writings, and I had already passed half of mine in a kind of absent-minded dismay, the heart everything, the head nothing. I was blessing my strong Lapland boots, which – despite the mockery of friends who are fans of espadrilles or flip-flops – I've been wearing for thirty years in all climates. For this 'sacred way', also regarded as a 'classical landscape' where people come to admire the full moon on inebriated trips to the country, no longer inspires the respect it deserves: the river-bed gleams with broken bottles; the path is dotted with dry turds, over which slender columns of blue flies buzz without much hope. *The old shit-track again!*

A bit later: 'Yangban'

Already within sight of the monastery, we caught up with a bow-legged old man climbing unsteadily, furiously striking stones with his cane, as though he wanted to punish them. Boiled-leather slippers, billowing white trousers, belted white tunic and a comic black-horsehair hat with a brim (somewhere between a top hat and a boater), which is – in the fields as in the town – the monopoly and pride of the functionaries or minor dignitaries of the former royal administration, the *Yangban*.

If I were a *Yangban* in present-day Korea I would take care to avoid boasting of it, and would rather pretend to be someone else. Throughout Korean history the members of this class of high civil servants and landowners were not noted for their competence or their virtue. The good dynasties often had to take them down a peg or two, and revoke their privileges. They cared enormously for appearance, and very little for the citizens whom they cheated. A fifteenth-century encyclopaedia describes them as corrupted by bribes and oppressors of the peasants: 'Fathers and mothers suffer from cold and hunger... cries of resentment rise to the heavens.' In the country, these survivors of grumpy Confucianism and a bygone order are still marked out by their haughtiness and pretension. The farmers who work their lands secretly think they're fools but treat them gently. During the thirty-five years of Japanese occupation their conservatism and ultra-chauvinism had been especially noticeable in contrast to the liberal attitudes of the Christians.

The *Yangban* are like turkey-cocks, raising their voices and using their canes to get themselves the best seats on buses or in cafés, more often than not inflamed by a combination of arrogance and alcohol. I even think that it is they who, after drinking, pull down their trousers no matter where, and soil this magnificent countryside. You could not find a more insufferable lot in any corner of Asia.

The one staggering ahead of us, a white streak under a white sky, was worthy of his fellows. He stank of *choshu*, a potato-based spirit which takes the top of your head off. He muttered a greeting, leaning forward to peek into Eliane's blouse, and had to clutch my arm to avoid falling over. A few steps farther on – he was walking beside me – he stuck his finger into my left ear without any warning and then stopped to look at the end of it, somewhat puzzled. In Korea, as in Japan, ear-wax is not solid as in the West, it's a fine dust which you brush away with a tiny feather duster. Without getting on my high horse (which you mustn't when travelling), and even if this were a legitimate ethnological curiosity, I found his gesture a shade too familiar. A vet would have gone through more formalities. He seemed set to follow us to the inn and drink there at our expense. I threw him off by taking his photograph up close. Koreans, especially the old, hate having their photo taken by strangers, fearing that their picture might then be used for nefarious purposes. At the third click he covered his face with both hands and hurried off towards the river bank, shaking with giggles and farting like a trooper.

Haeinsa III

In front of the monastery portico lies a square of beaten clay. At the grocer's, between earthenware jars of pickles, plaited garlic and peppers, and bunches of medicinal plants, the owner swats flies as he waits for a customer. In the joint next door, half a dozen *kiseang* (singers and prostitutes) are waiting, too. The road up from the plain has just been opened to traffic again, and you never know when a car of party animals might arrive. One of them dances by herself, transistor radio in hand, fag-end stuck to her lips, her eyes full of tears. The others kill time with games of mah-jong and rasping flirtatiousness. Awakening from an illusion: in yellow Asia, brothels and temples have always been good neighbours. The older women wear chignons and are made up in the old-fashioned way: a foundation that emphasises the cheekbones, plucked eyebrows re-shaped as half-moons; the young ones' faces are in the style of silent films: Cupid's-bow lips and lashes curled with a curling iron. All of them tough as old boots, more callous than crows.

When our friend from the riverbank arrives, having slept it off, it won't take them long to put some life into him and get him back on his feet.

Haeinsa IV

> To live under a tiled roof
> as big as a whale
>
> > (Korean definition of the good life)

Above the red-cedar columns which support the monastery's first portico, you see the 'guardians of the South', horned, armoured, brandishing two-edged swords or tridents and painted in garish colours.

Their motionless gestures and frightening expressions make children laugh, and are effective against not only djinns and demons but also envy, vulgarity, violence and haste.

The weariness of the journey makes me susceptible, open to the language of a place: it's impossible to cross the threshold without feeling lighter, cleansed of something. Directly above us the terraced monastery courtyards are paved with broad stones; the grey tiled roofs of the surrounding buildings rise in silence up the slopes of Mt Kaya. Masses of greenery. Nothing stirs. No one.

Where Buddhism of genuine quality has been established for a very long time, it brings a special kind of peace, both ethereal and weighty. It still prevails here, and its healing virtues soon work on the traveller's spirits. A few steps in, and everything suddenly becomes peaceful, noble, auspicious. One also has the impression of being mistaken about the century, not because of the thousand years of history and the age-old trees but because, once in the square, everything everyday, everything current seems to wake up and stretch, as if after a hundred years' sleep, as in a fairy-tale.

Indeed, on the low wall which borders the first level, an old man is sleeping, his arms crossed over his stomach, a red scarf across his eyes. There is a hint of rain, and the drops spattering his spotted hands don't cause him to bat an eyelid. Next to him a camera also rests, on its tripod, with a pear-wood case polished like a Stradivarius. A marvel from the last century, bearing the stamp of a cabinetmaker on the Quai Malaquais, Paris, and a 150mm Angenieux lens, its fittings all brass, worthy of the Niépce Museum. It is covered with plastic and placed on the north-south axis in order to take in the whole monastery and the mountain peaks, as a backdrop for honeymooners, school parties, political receptions or those gangster families who come here to perform the ceremonies of repose for the souls of rival gangsters they've just bumped off. As in Japan, the mafia here have great respect for their friends the bonzes. They envy their serenity, the spirit in which they approach all those pleasant tasks – chopping wood, polishing the cooking-pots used for rice, picking vegetables and mushrooms, weeding round the roses (Korean monks are mad about roses) – which they undertake without haste, carefully, in the hours they are not devoting to their beautiful liturgy, study or meditation. The bosses often leave considerable sums to Buddhist priests, gifts received as simply as they are given. Buddhism has never been eager to share our sense of right and wrong in this 'world of illusion', and considers that living in the underworld with its violence and prostitution is, in the end, just one more kind of suffering. Added to which conversation with these gangsters is often instructive, they know about all sorts of schemes and, however enlightened he may be, a good abbot can never know too much. Finally, as a medieval Japanese saint (Honen? Shinran? I can't remember now) wrote: 'If even a good man can be reborn in the Pure Land, how much more so a wicked man!'

… The old man wakes up, sits up, rubbing his eyes. We talk for a moment about apertures and emulsions. He hasn't seen anyone all day long. On the terrace overlooking us, monklings in grey robes play football with woodcutters come down from Mt Kaya, who had left their sleds laden with enormous bundles of wood up against the wall. They all play barefoot. Their ball is a large bundle of rags. Their game makes less noise than the cicadas.

Haeinsa V

Under the Yi dynasty (1392–1910), this inn east of the temple must have been a pavilion for royal guests. A glazed tile roof, curving up at the corners, and an oval doorway in the purest Ming style, over which hangs a Second Empire mirror (the remains of a French-style hairdresser's salon, destroyed by bombs?) at an angle that enables travellers to catch a glimpse of themselves entering into this image from a folding screen and congratulating themselves. A paved interior courtyard surrounds a well, where we wash our faces in icy water, and a pedal sewing-machine with a pattern of black and gold vines, lit up by the setting sun. Balconies of ornate blue wood. The tiny room overlooks a pond: bulrushes, lotuses, red dragonflies, and a team of ducks whose karma causes me no anxiety. Pleasantly tired out by the day, we watch them shaking their tails, while the vibrations of the monastery gongs, unhurried, make their way to us. Everything comes together in this moment, exactly, exquisitely, tuned like a lyre.

Haeinsa VI

Three hours' walk beyond the monastery, at the top of a bush-covered peak, there is a seven-metre-high stone Buddha, erected in the ninth century. The forest that has grown up since completely conceals it. The statue wasn't on any itinerary. We kept losing our way in the steep undergrowth, crossing the clearings where the wood-cutters of yesterday had slept under the stars amidst their huge faggots. Two nuns from the monastery gathering fungi in the forest set us on our way. We found it. It is sculpted from a red stone so hard that eleven centuries of bad weather and the wind that blows continually here have scarcely worn its features. Korean Buddhist sculpture of this period is one of the most expressive in Asia. The face sparkled with mischief and radiated compassion: at least it had the air of having understood – having always understood – our torments and frustrations, and of being inclined to give a helping hand. One could perceive, in this leafy silence, a clear trace of holiness. We almost heard him say, 'Give up worrying.' We gazed at him for a long time. Descending, I turned round to look at him several times: he followed us with his eyes, as I thought he would. It's true that he wouldn't have received many 'overseas' visitors.

For two months, I had given up worrying. Never, in Japan, had I worked in such agreeable company nor so well. My beloved wife had been able to join me. We were here for a while yet, without a programme or projects from day to day. When she returned to Europe, I would still have enough time and money to nose around Asia and fill in some of the blanks on my map. That's what I said to myself on returning to the inn, kneeling by the window, looking at the darkening pond. I also said that a Korean poet would undoubtedly add a frog to his *sijo* (brief eulogies of nature in three lines, a bit like Japanese *haiku*), to win over all his readers. And right on cue a frog began to croak. The world was complete.

In the bus from Deokam-ri to Gwangju
9 a.m. to 11 p.m.
Overcast sky, muggy, hills with their pale-green fleece of trees. Flooded rice-fields between them, all being planted: long lines of curved figures in their coloured skirts; scarecrows already set up, with their distressed gestures. It is very beautiful and indescribably sad – or perhaps it's tiredness from yesterday playing a trick on me. The road is dreadful; at the back of the bus we are tossed all over the place. Over three passes, not very high or steep for those who know the Alps, but oh so dangerous because the road twists over clay slippery with rain. We passed the previous day's bus fallen on its side in a rice-field, half-submerged, empty. It hadn't fallen from a great height, a good metre and a half at most, but just far enough to imagine (it must have been packed) dislocated jaws and shoulders, passengers knocked out, covered in shit (the rice-fields are covered with the contents of the toilet), angry, with trays of eggs broken on the peasant women's white clothes, those immaculate garments whose whiteness – how do they manage it? – they are so concerned about.

Kochang, towards midday
Grumbling roused me from drowsiness. A man enveloped in a cloud of flies was getting on the bus despite the driver's attempts to stop him. Under his arm he had a parcel wrapped in newspaper, stinking so abominably that for an instant I thought that the sun had darkened behind the fine layer of clouds. If it had not been for the continual rain and the fact that we were in the middle of nowhere, we would have got off and continued on foot.

Above the driver swung a clumsy drawing for our edification, showing the fate that awaited those who spied for North Korea: three merry peasants bearing a skewered, bloody body on the end of a pitchfork. The caption at the foot of the picture, in Hangul

(Korean script) and the same blood-red, probably indicated the amount of the reward.

There is incessant infiltration by agents and saboteurs; not a day goes by without one being caught, and hatred and fear are so strong that they rarely make it to the police station alive. The better for them.

Namwon, end of the afternoon
She was a sturdy, ageless woman. When I saw her arrive at the far end of the square, I couldn't believe my eyes: she was carrying an enormous pedal sewing-machine on her back, secured by a band across her forehead. The physical strength of Koreans, like that of Turks, is proverbial: all the same, with the base it would have weighed at least 80 kilos… and to get on the bus with such a huge object! She was one of those august mechanics in the – what shall we call it? – Ptolemaic style, who could keep a whole family and was worth her weight in gold. It would be a long time before she and her machine were separated. Pushing past, pleading, threatening, using her head and her haunches, bursting into tears, she nevertheless managed to get her burden to the bench at the back where we squashed up to make room. She sat down, sighing '*Aï! Chuketta!*' ('Whew! I'm done in!') then, having succeeded in her objective, she began to smile…

Even without such a load, the Koreans burst into tears over the smallest thing. The next moment they have forgotten it all; the earth is back on its axis. Then they chat to their neighbours, crush a louse found in a seam or squeeze a blackhead on their nose. In spite of being able to announce the death of a father with a smile and being harder than flint, the smallest trifle – elegiac evocation of frustrated love or crescent moon – will bring them to their knees. Twenty centuries of rigorous Confucianism have no doubt starched and stiffened them but without changing their essential nature. A quick people: lyrical, jugglers, emotional, undone by the slightest thing. Then they recover immediately: their tears are hardly dry before they set off again at top speed. Coming from Japan, you must get used to this mobility, since no Koreans are ashamed of it. *Nun-mul de opnum saram* (a man who does not know how to cry) is not trustworthy, is actually black-hearted, a good-for-nothing. And it's certainly not that they lack nerve: no people in Asia have come through such an atrocious war and kept so much punch and spirit. They discharge electricity by crying, like some fish or electric eels. You should see how refreshed and fulfilled they seem afterwards.

Gwangju bus station, 11 p.m.
Eliane had only just got off the bus when she was surrounded by half a dozen fifteen-year-olds, pulling her this way and that (probably towards 'their' inn), while another rogue tried to unbuckle her pack. I dispersed them by slapping their heads, elbows and knees with the resignation of a dead-tired man. They followed us, hurling insults and bottles, all the way to the hotel. I was happy to find one open at that hour.

Jeju Island
June 1970
A long time ago, Jeju emerged from the sea in a cloud of steam, sulphur and magma, bombarding the sky with white-hot rocks and unseemly trumpeting.

The eruption was powerful enough to create a volcanic cone nearly two thousand metres high and for about twelve hundred square kilometres of land to emerge.

Trade winds, monsoons, seeds, pollen, bees, birds – the island was soon covered with forests, pastures, azaleas, ferns, and the ocean warmly welcomed this velvety green newcomer.

Some centuries before the Christian era, men arrived from the peninsula – which is only two or three days away with a good wind – and settled down there, by one of the best seas in the world for fishing.

A matriarchal, shamanic society, this little independent kingdom which the Korean chronicles called T'amna entered into recorded history in AD 477, when it sent a gift of fine pearls, amulets and pheasants to the court of Paekche (on the south-west coast).

In 1276, the Mongol Kublai Khan deforested half the island in order to construct the fleet intended for the invasion of Japan, and introduced horse-breeding for his squadrons.

Three centuries later, the volcano went to sleep; the plume of smoke from its top, which identified its whereabouts from the coast, disappeared. Jeju, no longer seen, was forgotten.

In 1948 the island, which had claimed autonomy throughout its history, rose up against the loathsome and loathed government of Syngman Rhee. Seoul sent troops. The fighting lasted two weeks and caused twelve thousand deaths among the insurgents.* In these confrontations, the islanders had one advantage over the mainlanders: they spoke the only dialect on the whole peninsula that the Koreans didn't understand. Today, calm has been restored. The volcano is called *Halla-San* (Mt Halla).

Quelpaert Island, 1628

In this year, a Dutch merchant vessel is shipwrecked on the south coast of Jeju. Eight of those on board are rescued and taken care of by the inhabitants, who give them a warm welcome. The Koreans are too hospitable – and curious – to kill or bully men of an unknown race with whom they have no bone to pick. Those shipwrecked see that the island is a volcano, that the horses and everyone on it are free, that there are women who dive down twenty metres to collect pearls and shells, and that those who are devotees of magic hold some of the power. What they can't see is their position on a sea-map which the West hasn't yet drawn. They know that they are between China and the south coast of Japan where, two years earlier, one of their frigates had bombarded the castle of Shimabara and helped the Japanese wipe out the last of St Francis Xavier's Catholic flock. Since the campaigns and massacres led by the Duke of Alba in the Low Countries, they had had an account to settle with Spain. They didn't know anything more about the island, and named it – without going far inland – 'Quelpaert' ('Somewhere'). Once they had recovered, the Governor of Jeju sent them to the court in Seoul, where they taught the rudiments of martial arts and ballistics, and nearly

---

* The *Encyclopedia Brittanica* states that the rebellion began in April 1948 and that government forces did not regain control until 1949, with sporadic fighting until the early 1950s. Also that official investigation estimated more than twenty-five thousand were killed over the course of the fighting. (Trs.)

killed themselves trying to manufacture muskets. The Koreans remembered the name of one of these men: Wettevree.

Twenty-five years later, another Dutch vessel is driven ashore on Jeju by a typhoon. All on board who are saved – some thirty men and their captain, Hendrik Hamel – receive the same welcome, are revived, bandaged and sent on to Seoul, where they are politely begged, all else being set aside, to… make muskets.

Eight years later, Hamel and some of his crew manage to escape aboard a boat which sets them down at the Dutch trading-post of Deshima in Nagasaki harbour, from where they return to Europe. Hamel's memoirs were published in Paris in 1670: *Relation du naufrage d'un vaisseau hollandaise sur la côte de l'Ile Quelpaert*. It is he who put 'Quelquepart' on our maps and provided the first description of this brilliant 'hermit kingdom' which the West knew nothing about, and about which Marco Polo, who gave it the Chinese name 'Kaoli' (a corruption of *Koryo*, our 'Korea'), had written only a few lines.

The interesting thing about these two shipwrecks is the musket refrain. The Koreans had had to give way before Hideyoshi's arquebuses; they wanted to equip themselves to face any new invasion on an equal footing, and above all to regain the land the Chinese still occupied south of the Yalu River.

Of all the things that the West offered the refined cultures of China, Korea and Japan from the sixteenth to the eighteenth century, only two seem to have aroused their envy: firearms and astronomical instruments; and the industry, energy and curiosity with which the Society of Jesus was so amply endowed in those days. The Jesuits in Beijing, such a great source of knowledge about China, quickly understood that to be successful, their mission would one day have to include the production of sophisticated clocks (preferably with chimes) and of guns. When the Kangxi emperor issued his 'Edict of Toleration' in 1692, by which the Jesuits were permitted to exercise their ministry freely throughout the Empire, it was partly in recognition of their skills as arms manufacturers: 'During the civil wars, they [the Jesuits] rendered me a vital service by means of the cannon they cast' (cited by René Étiemble, *Les Jésuites en Chine*).

Ko, Yang and Pu

The three deities of the island are called Ko, Yang and Pu. Pu, as you can tell by the sound, is the god of farting. Coarse effigies of him, hewn from lava – nose running, huge legs, eyes bulging – are reminiscent of pre-Columbian idols. The island is the daughter of a marine fart: the original eruption.

'Ugh!'

'Why ugh? The Koreans don't find this analogy at all improper. Far Eastern traditions have never looked down on the body and its functions; rather, they consider them companions in work and pleasure which must be treated considerately, even, as in Indian Tantrism, as a means to spiritual knowledge. It's impossible to blaspheme or insult – as in the Judaeo-Christian or Islamic West – by using physiological vocabulary. If you call a Japanese man a "bum", you will see his eyes widen: *oshiri* (the honourable posterior) is no more worthy of a blush than the arm, nose or leg. In his *Sketches (Manga)*, Hokusai depicts not only hilarious face-pulling competitions, but also farting contests, with their competitors bottoms-up, concentrating, their performance bursting out like so many stars. In popular Korean stories there's a lot of outpouring of one sort and another; Rabelais would be able to sign half of them. The body is not – as with the prudish Victorians or in the hateful literature of the sextons of the shitty Counter-Reformation – a bag of gall, an instrument of suffering, fall and damnation before that resurrection promised to the "happy few".'

'All the same! Such scatology… for a founding myth…'

'Don't be so squeamish. Remember the materials Gargantua used to rebuild the walls of Paris, and recall that right up to the nineteenth century, Europe was carefree about farting, from Stockholm to Madrid, from farm to court, from cellar to attic. Reread Saint-Simon, Restif de la Bretonne, Sade, Chamfort, Rousseau; then you will wonder how, against such a cannonade, Haydn and Mozart made themselves heard. It was, I think, the young Queen Victoria who forbade this noisy practice at her court. From England the silence then spread across Europe – which I welcome.'

Somewhere: tombs

The Dutch chose a very good name: a hundred kilometres south of the coast and this isn't Korea any more. Neither is it the China of Shandong, six times farther away. It is 'Somewhere'. But find me another island where a little twin-engined Fokker, bumping like a taxi through the clouds, puts you down between grazing horses, small, narrow stone cottages with broad thatches, and tombs. Such tombs! They are tumuli covered in the very softest, short green grass, often surrounded by low lava-walls, the lightest protection; they are delicate lungs, with no suggestion of degradation, punishment, *de profundis clamavi*; rather, an eternal siesta, and exquisite, long-awaited, well-earned drowsiness. Shamanic tombs, where the deceased's head is positioned to the east and, in the oldest, the wings of great birds – frigate birds, cormorants or Manchurian cranes – are placed on each side of the body to help the soul take flight. These graves are found all over the countryside, breathing imperceptibly in their green bliss, their gentle convexity. 'Welcome to your repose.' I will return to die here.

Halla-San

When you see it from the north coast, this island volcano takes the form of a sleeping buffalo. As it rises, it changes in nature and cover: first yellow sands, where tumbled lava has set in mad formations of phoenixes and dragons; then fields of rye and rice-fields like mirrors shining on the slope; a layer of sub-tropical forest; then broad pastures; then on the eastern flank a sort of bib which is a forest of alpine conifers; and finally the jagged edges of the crater on which, even in June, sparkling snow draws your eyes towards its height. This buffalo is lighter than pumice stone; the oval island floats in the light like beaten egg-white. We want to climb up this animal.

On the map, there are two tracks marked in black dotted lines (thus of poor quality) up to the summit. One starts from the western beaches; the other from the road that runs between the port of Jeju and Seogwipo on the south coast. That's the one we take, without making any enquiries.

So It Goes

Five a.m.
The sun had not risen; the path was not a path but a mighty lava flow hewn by rain, frost and wind into hundreds of huge blocks which you have to walk around, climb up and down, jump from one to the next when you have the space for a run-up. On either side of this giant's causeway, the forest and its thorny undergrowth, where orchids hang like Chinese lanterns, are so dense that you need a machete to advance one step. I didn't even have a knife. Thus we were forced to follow the exhausting path dictated by the lava, and go where the mountain allowed us. Deafening song of nightingales. From time to time a golden pheasant would start up from under our feet with the sound of gunshot, and fly unsteadily towards the thin strip of sky which was beginning to turn pink.

Nine a.m.
Four hours of climbing to cover scarcely the same number of kilometres. When the summit appeared through a gap in the foliage, it seemed to be farther away. At each jump our heavy backpacks flew up and thudded down on our backs. If the rest of the route was going to be this difficult, we wouldn't get far with such loads. In a clearing created by the lava, I concealed the packs under leaves at the foot of a tree, and then climbed to the first fork where I attached strips of white paper, unrolling them to the ground, so that we could find them on the way back. Here, night falls like a stone.

One p.m.
The undergrowth had thinned out. The lava gave way to broad pastures on a gentle slope, scattered with wild peonies and high groves of flowering azaleas. Below us, a wood whose resinous scent reached us in gusts. I'd been poisoned by shellfish the previous night. Vomiting, with thirst made all the more intolerable because we could always hear the rustling of water somewhere beneath our feet. On this emerald green volcano you won't find a cup of water; rain is absorbed by the porous lava, all the water is underground and circulates, almost within reach, via the channels created by successive eruptions. To drink it, we would have needed a pickaxe.

156

The liquid warbled round a bend underfoot, and our throats so dry...

Three p.m.

Sitting on the trunk of a fallen pine above the last forest and the last lava stones, I felt the sickness lose its grip, worn out just before the body; having done as much as it could, it scarpered. I heard the day tumble away in pieces inside me, like a glacier. A team of geologists equipped with ropes and crampons to explore the grottos which pit the crater had given us drinks, and never had water tasted so good: that day, the words 'thirst' and 'water' had put on their Sunday clothes. The edge of the crater was only about an hour away, but I knew I couldn't go any farther. I had to conserve my strength for the descent and I had seen, in Japan, enough of these little volcanic lakes nestling in a landscape like a felt hat dented by a fist. Too bad.

The spur where we sat looked over the whole of the east side of the island, the ports on the north and south coasts, Jeju and Seogwipo. At these two cardinal points, and over the whole round sea, you could see junks converging on the jetties, their sails patched like gypsy trousers. Off the coast at Seogwipo, the graceful double jet of a right whale. Below us, the whole of the path we had travelled: from the beaches to the rice-fields, from the forests to the fields with horses standing about as in children's drawings, or more like those missionary illustrations in the 'Pavillons noirs' series which they sold us at Sunday school to filch a bit of our pocket money, and which did so much to set me travelling. Monks' imaginary maps with little sailing-ships, sirens and tritons. Indeed you had to climb up here to feel the solitude, the indescribable splendour and insularity of this volcano set down in the China Sea like a stone by Hop o' my Thumb. And you would have to comb this blue and bronze sea for a long time to find two mortals as happy as we were. I was done, in both senses of the word: exhausted, and at the place where I wanted to be. My wife began to laugh.

'You look like a dying sherpa.'

She took a photo, and I did look like a sherpa at death's door.

So It Goes

Five p.m.

As night fell, we reached the first block of stone on the descent, where we'd have to watch every step, and at the idea of doing the whole route in reverse, Eliane began to cry. She was, none the less, a better mountaineer than I and had scaled ridges I wouldn't have dared. There are some moments when crying (not complaining or arguing, just crying) is the best response to the question posed: an internal outpouring that reconciles and renews. I was in front and heard weeping behind me while leaping from block to block like a chamois, with absolute certainty. When she came to the end of her tears we had reached the plateau with the azaleas; she was at peace, on form, scoured like a cooking-pot. The Koreans were right to say that 'a man who does not know how to cry is a good-for-nothing'. In the evening horses came from all directions, at an idle trot like schoolboys on holiday, to look at us between two bushes of dark flowers, or to nuzzle our armpits in a friendly way. When we reached the forest below, night had fallen, the way was soft underfoot. Between the treetops, enormous stars were pulsing.

Eight p.m.
Fifteenth hour of walking

I had found the strips of paper and was lifting up our backpacks when a white torch-beam blinded me. We hadn't heard so much as a twig snap; I should have been alerted by my sense of smell. The beam which had dazzled me travelled down to my feet, and we saw a short, sturdy, earth-coloured soldier, his cap worn low over his eyes, a sub-machine gun over his right shoulder and two grenades attached to his belt. He gave off a strong smell of beer and, still holding us at bay, began to speak at top speed into his walkie-talkie in a furious voice. I behaved myself: in Korea, small men who are furious and tipsy, armed or not, could be mortally dangerous. He shouted at us in rough Korean; I replied in Japanese and saw his expression clear and relax. He hung his machine-gun back on its strap, took a notebook out of his shirt pocket, and I saw him put a cross over two vertical lines. Those two lines were us...

...Twenty-two years earlier, after the Jeju revolt had been harshly put down, a hundred resistance fighters had disappeared from the crater with arms, munitions and explosives; despite all the tracking and searches undertaken since, they had never been found. Not even a mess-tin or gun-belt, a skull or shinbone. The lava labyrinth which connects the cone of the main eruption to the secondary vents which pop out on the flanks of the volcano had hidden them. They had obviously stashed away their arms and cleared off: those who knew the innards of the mountain could get themselves into open air almost anywhere. The disappearance of these rebels had made the Seoul government so anxious that, ever since, the east and west access to Halla-San had been under secret surveillance. Everyone who went up the mountain came down under suspicion of having enlarged this army of hostile shadows. Usually those who went up one side spent the night at the crater and came down the other side. No one ever went up and back down in a day, it was too tiring. Our foolhardiness had disturbed this pattern.

The soldier accompanied us as far as the road, hanging on to my arm so that he didn't sway too much. He'd been in his copse for ten years, watching the comings and goings, quite convinced that the crater had been deserted long before his arrival. But being the doorman of a volcano extinct for a thousand years, and watcher over a battalion of ghosts, was actually a cushy job, holding scraps of conversation with the geologists, ornithologists and hikers who made the climb. Easy work then, and no danger. The anxiety that was obviously gnawing at this dwarf, armed to the teeth, and which enveloped him in a dark aura, was of quite a different kind: his wife was about to give birth to their first child; she had been ill during the pregnancy, and he was afraid of losing his good wife in childbirth and finding himself a widower. Having said 'widower' – *otokoyamome* – he fixed us with his bloodshot eyes, blinking, as though we were the masters of his fate. We reassured him as best we could: Korean women are strong, childbirth is not an illness, the little maternity wards all over the place staffed by missionaries are excellent…

Arriving at the road, he seemed to have regained his spirits. It was as black as pitch and we were asleep standing up. The soldier waited with us for a car to pass on its way to Seogwipo, which was several hours away on foot. He whistled at a fisherman's van to stop, and ordered him in a threatening voice to take us right to the inn and find us a room there, then shook our hands ceremoniously and lurched away into the undergrowth, to listen to the night and watch over his shadows.

Seogwipo, 5 a.m.
Last night, litres of tea to kill off the bug, chewing over my happiness in the dark, reviewing the fabulous spectacle of the day behind closed eyes. We were too worn out to go to sleep. At dawn we went down to the port, just below the inn. Silently, the fishing boats were leaving their moorings. On the jetty we bumped into a grandmother, jouncing a little howler on her back, and met a wan student in felt slippers who was walking the sea-wall with granny-steps. His stained shirt collar was darned with string. He confided to us in Jap-English that he was there to mend his collapsed lungs, and then, with the jovial indiscretion of the Koreans, he asked Eliane her age.

'Thirty-seven.'

'Ahh... I thought you were much older,' he replied, somewhat incredulous and frustrated.

Having satisfied his curiosity, he left us, dragging his feet. It is true that after fifteen hours of walking the previous day, and especially with our Western faces, all ridges and wrinkles, angles and anger, we age faster than they do with their moon faces. I was happy that this wonderful escapade had left its mark on us. It was like a notch on the assassin's knife. If we don't give our travels the right to destroy us a little, we might as well stay at home.

> And, without delay – that is to say
> immediately – something else happens.
> Charles-Albert Cingria
Florides helvètes

Seogwipo, June 1970
Los Angeles & Geneva, spring 1990

An Eight-Year-Old's War

This essay was originally published in L'Arc Lémanique, *a magazine whose title refers to the region on the north side of Lake Léman from Geneva to Lausanne and Montreux (an* arc *is a bow). It centres on the estate belonging to Bouvier's maternal grandfather, the composer Pierre Maurice (1868–1936). Bouvier said that he adored his grandmother, who used to copy out her husband's compositions in 'one of the most beautiful hands I've ever seen'. While admitting that he never quite understood his mother's character, and suspecting that she did not understand his, he described his upbringing as affectionate. His father became director of the* Bibliothèque publique et universitaire *in Geneva; he was somewhat distant in Bouvier's childhood, but they 'understood each other very well' as adults. As his grandfather had done, Bouvier rebelled against the impeccably bourgeois family expectations, and in this essay we see the early indications of his wanderlust.*

'Animula vagula blandula...'

Hadrian*

To say 'arc lémanique' is to make a beautiful pairing. Faced with this combination of words, my mind immediately goes in two directions. 'Lémanique' is timeless. 'Bow', for me, is a childish word that flies straight as an arrow from earliest childhood to death.

I made bows of various kinds: first from green hazel, the kind a kid can make with a bit of string before he has a knife. You can easily tear a branch off a bush, bend it with whatever you have to hand and use it to send a few twigs about three metres away, before the wood slackens and sags like bacon rind. That's 'SALT zero', zero-degree aggression. You can't even hurt yourself, although other rustic weapons – cheap and badly designed – disfigure apprentice terrorists or amateur makers for life. Later, I made bows at a workbench, out of ash, boxwood, yew. That was another thing entirely. The feathered arrows, with well-balanced aluminium shafts, their tips filed to a sharp point, travelled a hundred and fifty metres. If I had been a better shot, I could have pierced – for love – the heart of our maid, or – in defiance – that of Genghis Khan or Calvin. With the exception of a crow skewered by pure chance in the fork of an oak tree (its open mouth bubbling for a few seconds), it was all just a dream. I knew too little of life to take it away so lightly, despite an enduring hatred – now founded on study – of crows. I knew nothing of death. Certainly I had seen the dying and some prettified remains, but they were sickly old relatives whom my mother would take me to visit; they couldn't even remember my name, and their disappearance seemed logical. The kind of logic that you find in books.

I had to wait until my nineteenth year to understand, while watching the death-throes of a rat in a Bosnian tavern, that it was all to do with pumping blood. A housewife making her double bed

* The Emperor Hadrian's farewell to his soul, translated by Byron as 'Ah! gentle, fleeting, wav'ring sprite…' (Trs.)

163

pumps around eighty litres of blood through auricles and ventricles. A rat, despite its small stature, will pump nearly as much when making its nest with all the frenzy of that breed. The passions and the music of Bosnia are equally a matter of pulsing blood. In the end, it's everything: if the millions of litres chased at each moment through our millions of chests suddenly turned round to see if they were being followed, all this redness would ossify in our arteries and this planet, for me at least, would have no reason to turn.

That Bosnian café in the early 1950s was horrible. Because of the neighbouring cement-works, the soiled tablecloths were covered with a persistent film of grey dust. The factory siren blasted at six o'clock. The workers drank large glasses of plum brandy and munched onions. Some were drunk before they started work; the odds were that someone or other would leave a finger-bone or a foot in the teeth of a machine. I myself was grey with exhaustion, having driven all night. And there was this rat running along the skirting board, going about his business, knowing no better than any of us which was the most profitable or the most urgent thing to do. The drunks threw their glasses at him to knock him out. A fragment severed his left carotid artery and he continued on his way, spraying the wall with blood at regular intervals like a message in Morse code, then he fell down, rolled on to his back to the cheers of the café, and died. When the pulsing blood that is our glory but also our weakness finds its way out internally or externally – through a sudden aneurism or the assassin's knife – it is best to know one's prayers by heart and make them short: one disappears quickly, even if it's while dancing.

A few years later, my father died of a ruptured aorta. He collapsed on the pavement coming out of a florist's, where he had bought some tulip bulbs. Leaving a red message on the pavement would have been at odds with his modesty and proverbial discretion. The robbery was thus entirely an inside job: many things in my family were and remain 'entirely inside' for better or for worse. I was not in Geneva when this difficult moment arrived for him. I didn't need a message, I had already received it and have not finished mulling it over.

About the bows and arrows of my childhood I really have nothing more to add.

When you say 'Lémanique', I immediately think of the compass rose on a late eighteenth-century map which you can see on the first floor of a café in Ouchy (Vaud). Of course it's about the winds off the Great and Small Lakes, winds called Séchard, Joran, Mölaine and Fraidieu, for example. I can name four of them although I should be able to name twenty. This map, with its red and black arrows, resembles the plans of great Napoleonic battles: these winds aid, hound, evade, veer, come head-on as they whip up squalls. This map is as complicated as the lake and its surroundings; many a freshwater sailor has lost his life because he can't make head or tail of it.

Then the word brings to mind some wine-growers' households – peasant, bourgeois and patrician – in which I spent most of my summer holidays between the ages of four and twenty. Again they are complex: fine, dull, stormy. No two were alike. Each had its associations, its particular preferences; traits of taste or speech which made up such a singular universe that it would be impossible to house them all in the same story. So I have chosen one of them: the one I knew best.

It is grandparents who furnish a childhood for us, while we are using blunt pencils to draw hunchbacked houses with chimneys always smoking, even under a scorching sun. (This smoke is also a way of filling blank spaces with fat swirls and avoiding the teacher's saying, 'You haven't put anything there.')

Our parents, busy with looking after us when we get chicken-pox, or re-sit exams, getting us to take our fingers out of our noses and suffering all the anxieties of seeing their worries grow as we do, haven't the time to sketch out this geography.

Our grandparents have left the dance; indulgent, self-indulgent, delightful in the moments they're available. And shooing us away with the back of the hand like blowflies when our repetitive, stupid or pompous – children are often pompous, fearing to displease – babbling gets on their nerves. No child argues with their right to do so. Without being at all upset, one goes off towards the attics, garrets, laundries made to receive the words one murmurs and makes up on the way. Or towards the garages where the barouches mope, no longer in use since the appearance of the Hispano-Suizas or the Delage coupés, their violet- and maroon-silk seats spewing out horsehair and the finest dust. There I would sit down on the coachman's seat with a cousin, her knees crusted with clay (she traps frogs in the swamp and then cooks them, watching them swell and explode, as in the fable), and say, 'You are George Sand; I am Chopin,' and take up the cracked leather reins, setting off for Chamonix. Because there is a book that we look at together face down on the carpet in the library, where one sees exactly this: George Sand, Chopin and a Monsieur Pictet seen from behind in a horse-drawn carriage climbing towards Chamonix. And Chopin, with his luxuriant hair, what a chancer! And of course it's only natural that one tries to slide a hand into the warmth of her tightly clenched thighs, and all this is so innocent that on hearing her say, 'But what are you doing?' one replies, breathing heavily as children always do when they lie, 'Nothing, nothing at all.' *So it goes.*

In this house in Allaman (in the Vaud canton), the dinner-bell would ring, with the urgency of an alarm, twice: at noon, and at ten past, to round up those children at the farm or the lake. At quarter past, everyone had to be at the table, with clean nails and combed hair. All the ground we covered, panting for fear of reprimand, belonged to my maternal grandfather. As I ran, I would say to myself – because it was the largest stretch of country I'd ever run through – 'Carabas, Carabas.'

I was wrong: my grandfather was not a marquis (like Carabas), he was the smallest baron that I ever knew on this planet.

Small: five feet four inches at most. I have to hand a photo in which he is wearing a panama, pinstriped tennis trousers, and a nankeen jacket. His favourite dog, an Irish setter with which he hunted woodcock, was almost as tall as he was.

Baron? My great-grandfather had been a Bonapartist, a prefect of Geneva and of Léman, then a baron under the Empire. Like many Genevans, he had believed in the benefits of republicanism, but had become disenchanted. He had done his best to prevent Genevans from travelling, by conscription, to die in Smolensk or La Berezina. He is often remembered in this little town. Switzerland doesn't recognise the right of its citizens to titles of nobility – so much the better. My grandfather 'the baron' thus only existed in letters that came from abroad, and for a few people in the village – nothing in our Constitution demanded this consideration from them but they liked to address him thus; the taste of the Vaudois for all forms of excellence – however empty and old-fashioned – being, as is well known, limitless.

He was also the smallest dead baron that I ever saw or will see in my passage through this deceitful world. I was seven or eight when he died, some years before the war. I was taken up to his coffin, in which he was no bigger than a boy of sixteen. His shroud of white linen was stained with the pollen of the white lilies beneath which he had almost disappeared. His bony features like a wax doll's, his thin mouth with the same irritated expression that I'd often seen at the table when my Tante Marguerite said grace, a ceremony which I believe he would have dispensed with. Beyond his extreme thinness, these made-up remains were not at all frightening. All the more because the death of my grandfather was no surprise: each year they had removed another piece of his stomach. At the end, he must have eaten less than a Stylite fed on locusts and literally died of hunger. The candles which surrounded him prefigured in their logical order the candles on the fir tree under which we hoped to find the gifts ordered from a catalogue a few months previously. Sitting up straight in an armchair, my grandmother – with her weatherbeaten gypsy's face, her carbuncular eyes – swung her right foot and gazed at the little baron in silence, with a conspiratorial, friendly air, beyond sorrow and out of reach. She was already thinking about the resurrection of the body and the reunion over which, for the twenty years of her widowhood, reality never cast a doubt. I heard the whisking of eggs in the kitchen below. The roads were icy and the whole family would be staying the night.

My grandparents were secretly married at the age of six then, properly, twenty years later. They had lived quite a threadbare bohemian life in Paris, where my grandfather studied with Fauré and Vincent d'Indy, then in Munich where he had written quartets, oratorios and operas played often enough, but whose success never led to fame. It didn't matter: the Bavaria of the Wittelsbachs (which it remained at heart) surrounded its artists with a respectful good fellowship which wasn't measured according to fortune or success. It was enough to have some manners and spirit, to love music or – better still – to compose it, to be very graciously received everywhere. They had spent the war years there, half-starved in a freezing dwelling, and then held a grudge against the France of Clémenceau and the

Treaty of Versailles. My mother, who was twenty in 1914, spent most of her time, angelically, removing lice from haggard, illiterate Russian prisoners, and bathing their feet – wrapped in rags and bursting with chilblains – with Lysol. Despite this pitiful closeness to men, she was so ignorant of the facts of life that one day when a nurse happened to mention the way we come into the world, she fainted, fell flat on the floor and narrowly avoided breaking her neck. Those were the ways of that world.

It should be said that my mother was educated in the old way and had never set foot in a school. For almost twenty years school came to her, in the person of a lady (she seemed older than Barbarossa to me when I saw her in 1938) with a jutting chin, eyes alight with malice, who taught her four languages, the piano, the exact location of the canvases and retables of the Flemish, Siennese, Spanish and French masters worth seeing, and a very good grasp of history. European history, of course. Not a word about the female body: ladies from this background were assumed to learn about their misfortunes soon enough. She wasn't the only one in this state: in the great Huguenot and Wilhelminian estates on Lac Léman, puritanical and Victorian, there were legions of these white geese who married without any idea as to how the spirit 'came upon' girls. They clung resolutely to the stork. Not only was eros absolutely forbidden, but a good part of our physiology was weighed down with a negative charge, considered a trial to be valiantly endured and often as the 'wages of sin'.

I don't judge this lady for her silence: it was what was expected of her. Even less because when, two years before the war, we went to visit this ancient female Socrates, whom my mother had so often spoken about, she presented my brother, my sister and me with a miracle, for which it would have been worth crossing the Red Sea. It took place in the little house in southern Bavaria, exactly like Hansel and Gretel's, which she had constructed out of gingerbread an hour before our arrival, solely for our amazement. Mademoiselle Godin was as lively as a weasel, unusually ugly, extraordinarily alert to people and to things. After the conventional embraces and a conversation in German of which we didn't understand a smidgin, she felt that we children were waiting for her to produce something that matched her magic chimney and her witch's appearance. Night had fallen. She said to us in perfect French, 'I also know how to speak to frogs, you'll see,' and began to chant, standing on the steps, '*Fröschen, Fröschen, Fröschen…*' and at intervals producing from the back of her throat – which you could see palpitating like a bullfrog – a deep croak. Dozens of frogs, toads and tree-frogs soon emerged from the shadows and invaded her balcony. They leapt on to her hands, her chignon, her shoulders, and created an unbearable concert. I forget what spell she used to send them away, laughing the while at the mob. I was speechless with pleasure and terror.

After the defeat of Germany in 1918, my grandfather returned to the fold. The normal run of things reclaimed this black sheep, whose family didn't understand the 'artist's life', and delicately dropped him into the patrician cradle of this huge house surrounded by hectares of wheat, woods, fields, which bordered the bushes on the bank of the Aubonne and the shores of the Grand Lac, causing bitter disputes with workers in their Sunday best who believed they had a 'right of way' or, even worse, the right to peel their sausages or salamis in the shade of a willow or a clump of rushes. We were charged, my cousins, my brother and I, with low-grade policing, and were thus yelled at by 'plebs', who had heard tell of Léon Blum, the Front Populaire and paid holidays. Obviously at that age I had no social or political conscience, but I didn't really understand why these picnickers bothered us so much and especially why the adults themselves didn't tackle these intruders. It seemed to me that my grandfather would have done wonders had he raised his hat before requesting 'these people' to take their lunch elsewhere. He would have made more sense to them than I did, not because of his landowning privileges, which were questionable and questioned at every community council meeting, but because his politeness was natural while ours, towards people stronger than us and of whose situation we knew almost nothing, was forced.

The summer after my grandfather's death there were lots of letters and visitors from Germany. We saw the Daimler in its grey and black coachwork draw up at the steps, crunching over the gravel, to let out women sparkling with jet, with high voices and cheekbones, and men in pearl-grey hats, their beards perfectly trimmed. It was the end of a dream; I felt the angst piercing these voices.

I remember the afternoon when I learnt how to swim, dive and keep my eyes open under water all at once. Everything happened at once, like a present, without my being forced or bullied by bigger boys. Without swallowing the water. I was crouched on the shore, trembling with cold and excitement. A hundred and fifty metres out, my grandfather's wooden boat, a large Breton-style fishing-boat, was swaying, brimming with parasols and straw boaters. The German voices carried across the white water. These were the last years before the 'Thousand-year Reich' and the disaster. Yes, in the waters of my first lake there was a drop of Germanic absinthe, a taste of *Götterdämmerung* and Wittelsbach degeneracy, mixed with the slender algae whose spear-shaped leaves rose up from the bottom where perch and baby perch swam around their roots in the luminous grey sand.

'Me, me, me, ME!' That's what I was saying quietly, through clenched teeth, chin buried in my chest, palms down on either side of the plate on the damask tablecloth, when I was about eight, in that great house, echoing and cool in that undecided turn-of-the-century style, behind its banks of hydrangeas, terraces, verandas, towering foliage of beech or maple, its round stone pool from which water was drawn for the table with a long-handled dipper; a house I would locate somewhere between Chekhov and Massenet. A huge, desirable residence where the summer would cast its cooling shade between two chords struck on the piano and the snap of a whalebone fan being closed. Coffee cups tinkled under the yellow-striped awning. The torpor of August, not a word. I hear the yawn stifled by a slender hand, followed by that of a setter worn out by the heat. Are you yawning too? And yet, things were exactly as I describe them.

'Me!' I had the light of battle in my piss-coloured eyes, I was the smallest one at the huge table and no one heard the protest of the cricket lost in the flour-bin.

'Me!' But if by a miracle they had allowed me to speak, I would have remained tongue-tied. My stories – that summer there were two otters which I went to watch each morning, cavorting and splashing about at the mouth of the Aubonne – and their stories – Chamberlain at Munich, or who was singing Hans Sachs at Basel? – had very little in common. I said 'me', I wouldn't have said 'us': they no longer climbed trees and I had decided, that year, not to grow any more. The only things I envied 'them' were staying up at night; escaping the tyranny of the Prussian governess who had complete control of the house and terrified us brats; and above all, knowing a vast amount of things that I didn't know. In that respect, I really wanted to be one of them. I might have been a dunce and seen my sky obliterated by corrections in red ink and blackened with exams to re-sit, but the acquisition of knowledge seemed to me, as soon as I learnt to read, a process as fascinating and natural as breathing to a yoga teacher or the crawl to a middle-distance swimmer. I expected also from this *gai savoir*, this joy of learning, access to privileges not ordinarily available to children of my age and height.

My first *thesaurus pauperum** wasn't the *Petit Larousse* that the peasants of the Auvergne or Haute-Loire used to leaf through to keep their memories in trim over the dead winter season, but a work published by the four Swiss chocolate manufacturers, *L'Album NPCK*, which combined the initials of the firms Nestlé, Peter, Cailler and Kohler. Today the first of them has taken over the other three – so it goes! You would send coupons clipped from chocolate wrappers to the publisher and receive a folio, *Great Figures of World History*, with blank spaces for the coloured pictures which were obtained by sending more coupons. I have never seen an undertaking of this kind – popular culture explained – done so well: to win their laurels these chocolate manufacturers must have employed a son of Dr Faustus to skim over the centuries, parallels and meridians without omitting a single important figure. The captions of about twenty lines under each figure gave all the information a ten to fifty-year-old could want. You reeled from Semiramis to Pasteur, from Sargon the Great to Stevenson, from Montezuma to Lao-Tsu and from Robert Surcouf to Thomas More as if intoxicated. My head expanded with pleasure, like the universe during the Big Bang, as the blanks in chronology and the Mercator projection were all filled with a fine hatching of grey, pink and yellow. The rough and ready

* The *Thesaurus Pauperum* (Treasury of the Poor) was a compendious medical dictionary, with remedies for every known disease of the body, compiled by Peter of Spain (Pope John XXII, d. 1334) in Latin and translated and adapted in many European languages. The *Petit Larousse* was first published in 1905, and consists of both a dictionary and an encyclopaedia of proper names, with illustrations and maps. (Trs.)

illustrations were not the work of Dr Faustus's son, but probably of his stable-boy. The three Chinese sages in the collection – Confucius, Mencius and Lao-Tsu – all had the same wispy, drooping moustache, the same snub features and were only distinguishable by the shape and colour of their hats. Catherine the Great and Empress Maria-Theresa shared the same disdainful expression, the same wig and were only differentiated by the colours of the thick ribbon they wore like a chain around their necks. Such Épinal-style images* at least had the advantage of making these demi-goddesses and demi-gods entirely accessible to children and ordinary people. I would have recognised Stanley and Livingstone in the street as long as they hadn't swapped their pith helmets for nightcaps. As I've said, it all rested not on expression – fleeting and unreliable – but on headgear, evidence of social standing and offering a more solid guarantee. A mandarin, it seemed, might have worn the wrong expression, but if he wore the wrong hat for a formal occasion, he was a lost man. I bless the author of this collection, which would still be useful today (I've forgotten so many details and dates since then), but I must have got rid of it in a moment of haughty adolescence, unless it fell to pieces, disintegrating in jam.

I had acquired the volume secretly, going to post the letters myself, and hadn't shown it to anyone. In the bathroom – for the smallest trifle, the sadistic Prussian Bertha would pitilessly purge the puny child that I was with an enema of black soap – I read with saucer-eyed attention those lives which had founded religions, cities, empires, monastic orders, saved or killed millions of children like me. I retained it all with the appetite and memory of that age, and also with the idea that this knowledge would allow me to catch out (being hypocritical and unfair) those 'grown-ups' who, besides the Italian Renaissance – on which subject, I don't know why (Burckhardt?),† they were unbeatable – knew a great deal less about this huge world than they thought. Because of excessive Eurocentrism – even among the most curious – and the absolute

---

* Épinal prints, images of popular subjects in bright colours, were sold in France in the nineteenth century. The phrase *image d'Épinal* now means a naïvely positive depiction. (Trs.)

† Jacob Burkhardt was a Swiss historian of art and culture whose best-known book, *The Civilisation of the Renaissance* in Italy (1860), transformed the view of the Renaissance. (Trs.)

domination of Judaeo-Christianity, other traditions and cultures were relegated to being accessories in the bazaar, confined to the roles of foil, reflection and reference for our passing fancies, but refused any real existence or independent substance. China was a folding screen, Egypt a hieroglyphic scarab. One knew about the Jews, but not the Amalekites. One knew all about the Crusades and nothing about the Mamelukes, and if they could quote Stanley, Marchand, Father de Foucauld and Kipling, they were not interested in the Sudan, Algeria, Cochinchina or India except in so far as there were Protestant missions there to which they gave donations. And if these people who featured in my bible were familiar to them, it was also because they were considered 'courageous'. In this summer residence, courage was the virtue most often commended. Its praise literally oozed from the *toile de Jouy* and sombre panelling of the library. This courage, let's be clear, could only be military, alpine or passionate. Edward Whymper and Lord Kitchener were courageous. Madame Caillaux, too: she had killed to avenge her husband. It couldn't be civic: Zola, who had risked his life in writing *J'accuse*, which facts had proved right, was rather 'badly brought up'. Rathenau, assassinated by pan-Germanists who paved the way for the Nazis, 'didn't understand Germany'. Etcetera.

Madame Caillaux – almost uniquely – was not in the album thanks to which I soon managed my first breach of the adult front. That midday, there was a couple from Munich whom I liked very much seated at the large oval table: he was a Board member of the magnificent Deutsches Museum; his wife, a Romanian princess crazy about Buddhism, had chosen the inverted 'swastika' for Adolph Hitler as the symbol of his party.* Like many of their peers, these Bavarian humanists had been mesmerised by the Führer, without having read *Mein Kampf*, without weighing up the danger that Nazism posed for the West as well as their own country. All the more bewildering and bizarre in that they had many Jewish friends, including the violinist Ysaÿe, the conductor Heinrich Porgès and dissidents such as Thomas Mann's family. Neither racists nor anti-Semites, but viscerally anti-Prussian. When their eyes were finally opened to the crimes of their protégé at the end of the 1930s, he was

---

* Hugo Bruckmann (1863–1941), a publisher, and his wife Elsa (1865–1946) held salons at which they introduced Hitler to the higher echelons of Munich society. (Trs.)

dying and Germany was in flames. After the defeat of the Reich, the Americans organised compulsory visits to Dachau for those of the elderly who had shared this blindness and who had survived. Elsa Bruckmann, née Cantacuzene, died of a stroke several days afterwards. *So it goes.*

This couple didn't have children, and treated those of other people with the politeness and attention that is reserved for the keepers of lost magic, or the only plausible authors of the tales of Grimm or Andersen. This gave us the right – which we didn't usually have – to ask them questions at the table. That morning I had seen in the newspaper in which I was following the war in Spain (in the absence of a radio which was thought subversive and of television which didn't yet exist, my cousins, my brother and I gorged ourselves on print like invalids) the photo of an eleventh-century corpse found in a Jutland peat-bog, as perfectly preserved as an Egyptian mummy. He still wore around his neck the leather thong with which he had been strangled before they got rid of him. I asked the knowledgeable old man whether the Hanseatic League was already in existence at that time. He laughingly replied, 'It's as if I'd asked you what was happening in China at the end of the thirteenth century!' I took my first arrow out of the *NPCK* quiver, and replied without lifting my nose from my plate: 'The Mongol Kublai Khan had invaded it, established his capital in Peking, occupied part of Burma and Vietnam and launched an ill-fated maritime expedition against Japan. Marco Polo, who was in his service, recounted all this.' Bruckmann let out a roar of laughter; my grandmother flashed me an amazed and avid smile; my father's hazel eyes glanced at me with complicity and amusement, as though he guessed my tactic. He could certainly have responded rather than me but, for reasons which escape me even today (perhaps anxious at being thought frivolous), he carefully concealed the extent of his knowledge. Via this little cultural penalty point, I managed to attack – without her suspecting a thing – one of the most hated figures of my childhood, Bertha, the Prussian warder, who with the cowardly complicity of the adults had made me (I was the youngest) her scapegoat and favourite punchbag.

Bertha had entered my grandparents' service in Munich, before the 1914 war. At that time and place, a couple of artists could economise with regard to gas lighting, candles, firewood, and play the piano with mittened hands in a glacial apartment, but it was inconceivable not to have the door opened by a maid in a white apron, whom they paid less than a farmhand. In the critical years of rationing, she showed unconditional devotion and, in the long queues that formed outside the food shops, was as efficient as a panzer in shoving, intimidating and aggressively reducing to silence the Bavarians whom she thought little of anyway, stomping past them and returning with a bundle of dried cod under her arm. Having been so helpful to my grandparents when their means were slight gave her, now that they were wealthy, discretionary power: she could rule as she pleased and terrify the little maids whom my uncles and parents brought with them, who spent their time wiping their eyes, shut up in the wardrobe. Bertha, who had grown like a black pearl in the oyster of the family, henceforward had charge of the entire territory. In the great houses of La Côte where we were taken as kids, on family or friendly visits, I met more of these 'pearls' who, over the course of the years, had gained an absolute hold over their employers, but by kindness and intelligence. These vestals in lustrous dresses often reigned as enlightened despots, equitably seeking the good of their subjects, interposing themselves between the little ones and the grown-ups' punishments. In short: tutelary presences with whom you could, under certain conditions, come to terms. Not so Bertha, whom power had turned bad and whose greatest pleasure was in punishment. A bitch can be at the same time devoted and bad. Or a sow: the winegrowers and peasants of the village of Allaman who distrusted her almost as much as I did called her 'Bismarck's sow' and winked when they spoke of marrying her to the boar.

Until my mother got married, Bertha had been her chaperone on her 'cultural' travels: pictures taken by photographers in the streets of Madrid, Venice, Dresden and Amsterdam showed them side by side: my mother looking submissive under her fringe; Bertha strong, athletic, hatted and corseted like a mountaineer, shooting a bovine look heavy with menace at the camera. The Carpaccios, Memlings, Patinirs, the works of Bramante that she must have regarded with the same eyes in the course of these expeditions had not managed to brighten her Spartan, rustic mind.

In her heart of hearts she had decided that the time for escapades had passed and that my mother must remain a spinster and devote herself entirely – like Bertha – to my grandparents; that is: read aloud Maeterlinck or Alexander Von Humboldt, arrange flowers to go on the two grand pianos and the Chinese chest of drawers that came from Versailles, take over the Sunday school for the village kids that she had taken for years and, if she had any leisure time, hem dishcloths while dreaming of a Prince Charming who would never arrive. I have something to say about this Sunday school: my mother knew the Bible almost off by heart, which is difficult. She was fiercely determined to put it into practice, which is impossible. To help with the evangelisation of the kids at school, she used, as well as her own tormented faith, a brochure published by the free Vaudois church. The third chapter began with three words that no one in the village, even the trustees, could understand: 'Islam sanctions polygamy.' Prince Charming? When my father, already bald, came along somewhat belatedly and removed her preferred companion and victim, Bertha immediately hated him. She must have been affronted not to go on the honeymoon. She considered this commoner a second-class son-in-law, and the fruits of this regrettable union (my brother, my sister and myself) as intruders in the house, just heads to clout, and she never missed an opportunity to let us know that. Shrewd enough to perceive what I thought of her stolen authority, she kept her eye on me especially, and – just one example of her harassment – would come along with her heavy tread and her smelly armpits to clean the piano keys with 'spirits of mint' every time I brushed them, even though for as long as I can remember I would never have touched a piano without washing my hands. That my mother had made a happy marriage – for so it was – only added to her resentment.

Returning to that lunch at which I began the pincer movement which would rid me of that rhinoceros, old Bruckmann discreetly sounded me out about my sources, and I was careful not to reveal their popular and commercial nature. He threw out random famous names about whom my who's who kept me perfectly informed, then others that were less well known: there too, my miraculous album kept me going. It was the name Odoric of Pordenone (1286–1331) that really hit the jackpot for me. Only my examiner and my father, who was more and more amused, knew what that meant. I gave a brief outline of his travels in India and China without changing my tone of the-innocent-prompted-by-angels. My Stakhanovite writer of the *NPCK* must have been a defrocked Franciscan, or in any case not taken a day off when it came to the chapter on the holy pilgrims of the Middle Ages. Alleluia!

As soon as I got up from the table, I went to get my bible from under the mattress to conceal it under an old tennis-net in the attic, certain that henceforth that Gorgon would no longer have a hold over me – the Dr Faustulus that I had become in the space of one meal – nor the right to lead me off by the ear, like a puppy who had forgotten himself. Moreover, I was in credit elsewhere: about a hundred coupons clipped from chocolate that I'd never eaten (I don't like it), which my lovely big girl-cousins had taken charge of devouring. There too, I hoped to have acquired, for future use, a little stock of indulgence even if it had no tangible outcome.

The moment of truth that I expected was not long in coming. The same evening I was on the terrace after dinner, knees under my chin, listening to the grown-ups talking about the coming of airships, after two zeppelins bursting into flame in Ludwigshafen and New York had transformed their passengers (only the jet-set) into mere puffs of helium. It was 1938 and I was nine. Bertha came to look for me to take me to bed, where she would tuck me in tightly, muttering threats. I then played my first joker and said, in a worldly way, in the dark, 'No, this is interesting, I'm staying.' As I had expected, she grabbed me roughly by the arm to tear me away from the still-warm step on which I was sitting. As I had only dared hope, I heard a voice ring out through the night, 'Leave him alone, he'll go to bed when he's sleepy.' The voice of my grandmother: when it came to standing up to Bertha, my mother was as if sedated. The Prussian, who had never been defeated on this ground, stood firm on her large feet, ready to do battle and to reel off the list of that day's violations of the code she alone had drawn up and knew. My grandmother replied drily that they would discuss it some other time and asked her to withdraw. She let go, gave me a look that did not promise well and disappeared, stomping off noisily. A vein pulsed in her thick red neck; she had aged ten years. Our war had begun. From that day onwards, I attacked her like the pinch of salt which gradually dissolves slugs. It took me three years of viperish manoeuvres to reduce her empire and her authority to ashes. I stripped it off leaf by leaf like an artichoke, without touching its heart (the stove), because she was an incomparable cook. 'Don't disturb Nicolas when he's working.' I had acquired an indisputable monopoly over my grandfather's piano, my grandmother's friendship – she never failed to support me – and the right to scamper from cellar to attic without anyone yelling or chasing after me. A little vengeance also for the insults that my father, for the sake of peace, had swallowed. I had won my war.

Meanwhile the real war – atrocious, stupid, unbearable – had broken out. The 'grown-ups'' war: I followed it with my finger under the lines of the newspaper, with dismay, without forgetting to rejoice in my own small victories. *So it goes.*

About the Author

The traveller is always an enigma. He is at home everywhere and nowhere. His is a life of stolen moments, reflections, minute sensations, chance discoveries, and odds and ends.

So wrote Nicolas Bouvier (1929–1998), who was born in Geneva; it remained his home base during a lifetime of travelling. The last essay in this collection describes how his passion for travel began, and his own cultured family that rarely looked beyond France and Germany for its defining experiences. Having been confined to Switzerland by the war during his adolescence, and after finishing his degree at Geneva University in 1953, Bouvier set off on his first odyssey, not waiting for his results. His travelling companion was the Swiss artist Thierry Vernet, and their journey in a Fiat Topolino across Yugoslavia, Turkey, Iran and Pakistan was recounted by Bouvier in what is now a cult travel book, *L'Usage du Monde* (*The Way of the World*), published in 1963. They parted at the Khyber Pass, and Bouvier travelled down through India to catch up with Vernet in Sri Lanka. He lingered on the island, and decades later found himself able to tell the story of those hallucinatory months in *Le Poisson-Scorpion* (*The Scorpion-Fish*), a story of 'negative enchantment'.

Meanwhile he had lived in Japan in 1955–6, working as a freelance journalist and photographer; again in 1964–6 on assignment for *Editions Rencontré*, this time with his wife and young son; and returned in 1970 as a writer and photographer at the Osaka World Exhibition. Out of long immersion and pleasure in Japanese culture came *Japon* (1967) and in 1975 *Chronique japonais* (*The Japanese Chronicles*). He was commissioned to travel and write – as in the pieces on Scotland in this volume – but also wrote after considered reflection on his experience, years after the events his essays describe. *Journal d'Aran et d'autres lieux* (1990) presents three places: Aran in winter, a solitary and feverish stay in 1985; South Korea in summer, a buoyant month's walking with his wife in 1970; and Xian, where he led a group of travellers, alongside a remarkable local guide.

Bouvier also developed a career as an *iconographe*, a 'stalker of images' – paid to find arresting illustrations by all sorts of organisations; his French biographer, François Laut, subtitled his book *'L'oeil qui écrit'* ('the writing eye'). Patrick Leigh-Fermor, introducing the first English edition of *L'usage du Monde*, appreciated Bouvier's distinctive qualities as a writer:

> Passionate curiosity, appropriate seriousness and a comic sense are kept in balance by a wide, tolerant and most unusual cast of mind. He has the intuitive gift of capturing landscapes, atmospheres and personalities in a flash, and he finds himself totally at home in the heart of heterodoxy and strangeness. […] he catches scenes and atmospheres with a painter's eye and a poet's ear.

His reputation has grown in the years since his death, and he is now regarded as one of the foremost travel writers of the twentieth century.

ELAND

61 Exmouth Market, London EC1R 4QL
Email: info@travelbooks.co.uk

Eland was started thirty years ago to revive great travel books that had fallen out of print. Although the list soon diversified into biography and fiction, all the books are chosen for their interest in spirit of place. One of our readers explained that for him reading an Eland is like listening to an experienced anthropologist at the bar – she's let her hair down and is telling all the stories that were just too good to go into the textbook.

Eland books are for travellers, and for readers who are content to travel in their own minds. They open out our understanding of other cultures, interpret the unknown and reveal different environments, as well as celebrating the humour and occasional horrors of travel. We take immense trouble to select only the most readable books and therefore many readers collect the entire, hundred-volume series.

You will find a very brief description of our books on the following pages. Extracts from each and every one of them can be read on our website, at www.travelbooks.co.uk. If you would like a free copy of our catalogue, email us or send a postcard.

ELAND

'One of the very best travel lists' WILLIAM DALRYMPLE

Libyan Sands
RALPH BAGNOLD
*An heroic account of an infatuation with the
Model T Ford and the Sahara*

An Innocent Anthropologist
NIGEL BARLEY
*An honest, funny, affectionate and
compulsively irreverent account of fieldwork
in West Africa*

Memoirs of a Bengal Civilian
JOHN BEAMES
*Sketches of 19th-century India
painted with the richness of Dickens*

Jigsaw
SYBILLE BEDFORD
*An intensely remembered autobiographical
novel about an inter-war childhood*

A Visit to Don Otavio
SYBILLE BEDFORD
*The hell of travel and the Eden of arrival
in post-war Mexico*

Journey into the Mind's Eye
LESLEY BLANCH
*An obsessive love affair with Russia and
one particular Russian*

Japanese Chronicles
NICOLAS BOUVIER
*Three decades of intimate experiences
throughout Japan*

The Way of the World
NICOLAS BOUVIER
*A 1950s road trip to Afghanistan,
by a legendary young sage*

The Devil Drives
FAWN BRODIE
*Biography of Sir Richard Burton,
explorer, linguist and pornographer*

Travels into Bokhara
ALEXANDER BURNES
Nineteenth-century espionage in Central Asia

Turkish Letters
OGIER DE BUSBECQ
*Eyewitness history at its best: Istanbul
during the reign of Suleyman the
Magnificent*

An Ottoman Traveller
EVLIYA ÇELEBI
*Travels in the Ottoman Empire,
by the Pepys of 17th-century Turkey*

Two Middle-Aged Ladies in Andalusia
PENELOPE CHETWODE
*An infectious, personal account
of a fascination with horses,
God and Spain*

My Early Life
WINSTON CHURCHILL
*From North West Frontier to Boer War
by the age of twenty-five*

A Square of Sky
JANINA DAVID
*A Jewish childhood in the Warsaw
ghetto and hiding from the Nazis*

Chantemesle
ROBIN FEDDEN
*A lyrical evocation of childhood
in Normandy*

Viva Mexico!
CHARLES FLANDRAU
*Five years in turn-of-the-century
Mexico, described by an enchanted Yankee*

Travels with Myself and Another
MARTHA GELLHORN
*Five journeys from hell by a great
war correspondent*

The Trouble I've Seen
MARTHA GELLHORN
*Four stories of the Great Depression,
offering profound insight into the
suffering of poverty*

Bangkok
ALEC WAUGH
The story of a city, a monarchy and a nation

The Road to Nab End
WILLIAM WOODRUFF
A story of poverty and survival in a Lancashire mill town

The Village in the Jungle
LEONARD WOOLF
A dark novel of villagers struggling to survive in colonial Ceylon

Death's Other Kingdom
GAMEL WOOLSEY
The tragic arrival of civil war in an Andalusian village in 1936

The Ginger Tree
OSWALD WYND
A Scotswoman's love and survival in early twentieth-century Japan